Sport Fishing in British Columbia

by Mary L. Peachin

Copyright © 2016 Sport Fishing in British Columbia All rights reserved

ISBN-13: 978-0991198146
ISBN-10: 099119814X

All rights reserved. No part of this publication may be reproduced, stored in a retrieval system or transmitted in any form or by any means, electronic, mechanical, photocopying, recording or otherwise, without the prior written permission of the publisher.

Printed in the United States of America

Cover photos: Mary L. Peachin and Owen Bird
Photo Editor: Chris Mooney
Interior Layout and Editing: Margie and Morgan Baxley

Table of Contents

Dedication — 8
Foreword — 9
Introduction — 13
Salt and Fresh Water Fish Species — 16
    Salmon
        Chinook
        Coho
        Pink
        Chum
        Sockeye
        Steelhead
    Sturgeon
    Trout
        Rainbow
        Cutthroat
        Bull
    Halibut
    Rockfish
        Rock Cod
        Ling Cod
    Albacore Tuna
Fishing Techniques — 19
    Mooching
    Trolling
    Jigging
    Fly Fishing
    Spin Casting
Department of Fisheries — 22
    Fishing Licenses
        Freshwater
        Tidal Salt Water

Certified Guides	23
Sport Fishing Institute	23
Pacific Salmon Foundation	24
What to Take With You	25
British Columbia: An Adventure in Travel	
How to Use This Guide	
British Columbia Lodges and Fisheries	27
Haida Gwaii Introduction	
Charlotte Queen Adventures	
Langara Fishing Adventures	29
Chinook Lodge	
Eagle Lodge	
Raven Cottage	
Alaska View Lodge	
Kumdis River Lodge	
Moosehead Lodge	
Maude Island Retreat	39
Naden Lodge	40
Peregrine Lodge	42
Queen Charlotte Lodge	45
Charlotte House	
Haida House	
Totem House	
MV Driftwood	
The West Coast Fishing Club	48
Westcoast Fishing Resorts	58
The Lodge at Hippa Island	
Englefield Bay	
Central and Northern British Columbia	63
Introduction	
Central Coast Adventures	63
Duval Point Lodge	65
Haa-Nee-Naa Lodge	67

Hakai Pass Lodge	69
Ole's Hakai Pass Resort	71
Nimmo Bay Resort	73
Prince Rupert Foggy Point Charters	75
Shearwater Resort and Marina	75
Sund's Lodge Malcolm Island	77
West Sport Fishing Lodge	90
Great Bear Rainforest	104
Westcoast Fishing Resort's Milbanke Sound Lodge	105
Westwind Tugboat Adventures	111
Rivers Inlet	113
Introduction	
Black Gold Lodge	113
Duncanby Lodge	116
Legacy Lodge	118
Sportsman's Club	123
Fly Fishing Destinations	127
Introduction	
Lower Dean Fly Fishery	127
Hodson's Dean River Lodge	127
Kimsquit Bay Lodge	130
Lower Dean River Lodge	132
Skeena River	135
Skeena River Lodge	135
Skeena Spey Fishing Lodge	137
Elk River	138
Introduction	
Fly Fishing in Fernie	
West Chilcotin	142
Introduction	
Langara's Moosehead Lodge	144
Stewarts Fishing Lodge	147

Vancouver Island	154
Introduction	
Critter Cove	156
Homefray Lodge	156
Dolphins Resort	158
Kyuquot Sound Lodge	160
Nootka Island Lodge	165
Rugged Point Lodge	168
The Lodge at Gold River	171
Tofino: the King of Tides	173
Lower Mainland	180
Richmond, British Columbia's Gateway to Sport Fishing	
Contributors	192
About the Author	193

Dedication

Thomas "Tom" David Bird

A sportsman, marine biologist, husband, and father, who worked tirelessly and passionately to protect and promote sport fishing in British Columbia. His many years of dedicated service to the public sector were matched only by his time and energy devoted to exploring and fishing our province's coast. Dad missed few opportunities to wet a line, whether it was with his wife, Carol, me, or family or friends, new and old.

Owen and Carol Bird

Foreword

British Columbia Sport Fishing is an excellent guidebook for those who would like to experience our fresh and tidal fisheries, as well as those who have previously enjoyed them almost as much as I have.

While Mary L. Peachin has spent more than a decade exploring our fisheries, I was raised with them surrounding my backyard. Born in Vancouver, I was a toddler when my father, Tom Bird, first introduced me to fishing. Back in the 70's, during the Georgia Strait glory days of abundant coho and Chinook fishing, I used a rowboat off Bowser beach, just north of Big Qualicum River on Vancouver Island. Like my father, my mom, and Carol, I became passionate about sport fishing and remain so to this day.

I spent every summer fishing first in that rowboat and later in a small whaler that allowed me to fish nearby Hornby and Denman Islands. Whenever possible, the entire Bird family shared the experience. Following summer workdays at Deep Bay Auto Court and Fishing Camp, I fished using raked herring with a couple of ounces of weight down 10 to 20 pulls in depth to pursue bountiful coho, Chinook, and pink salmon. Exposure to this environment and the ever-present attraction of fishing made an indelible impression on me.

There was very little opportunity to fish while attending college, but following graduation, I was able to use my previous experience to secure a job as a fishing guide in Haida Gwaii. From that point, I would seal my fate and commitment to sport fishing in British Columbia waters. The people, environment, and of course the fishing in Haida Gwaii was absolutely beyond compare. While Georgia Strait had laid the foundation for my growing appreciation of sport fishing, it was the opportunity to fish in remote regions of our fantastic province that settled the score. I happily spent the next six years guiding during summer months and travelling and fishing in locations all over the world during the other months of the year. The more I travelled, the more it became clear to me that I had a growing knowledge and a very real bias. I realized that while there were many beautiful and productive fishing locations around the globe, none were better than British Columbia. I still feel that way.

While a guiding career satisfies many when it comes to fishing, I found myself increasingly interested in encouraging participation in and sharing my love of the sport with others. I also wanted to become involved in the work of protecting fishing opportunities and the natural resources. I produced internationally broadcasted television fishing shows for nearly a decade. During that time, I was fortunate to fish extensively in the Province and around the globe. Once again, I arrived at the same conclusion I had when I was a backpacking angler and guide; what we have in British Columbia is second to none. Ten years of producing a television show is a pretty good run in show business terms but it came to an end. I found myself well positioned to work with a group of dedicated individuals who are committed to protecting the rights and opportunities of anglers and our fisheries resources.

Still, the love for sport fishing in British Columbia's waters was instilled in me at a very young age. That feeling continues to guide my activities in work and life. I am now hopeful that I can inspire my son, not unlike the way my father did for me, and that my son will be able to enjoy a whole set of his own fishing experiences and opportunities throughout his lifetime.

I am very pleased to have been given the opportunity to provide this foreword for Mary's book about fishing in British Columbia. Mary is a longtime sport fishing angler, one who has been drawn to saltwater billfish and tarpon, as well as fly fishing. When my father, the late Tom Bird, heard about her and the many award-winning fishing articles she was publishing in major United States fishing magazines and newspaper, it didn't take him long to "hook her" on British Columbia fisheries. Primarily a "catch and release" angler, whether ocean or stream fly fishing, it was years before she took home a lodge's flash frozen filet of salmon or halibut.

One of a minority of fishers who is also passionate about scuba diving, Mary uses her expertise as a photographer to further enhance the quality of this guide. She quickly abandoned Alaska's fishing and as she further explored British Columbia lodges and rivers, the gateway of Vancouver became a magnet, a city that aroused her curiosity.

Not a fan of large cities, Mary became captivated by Vancouver's beauty, culture, attractions, and cuisine. Her fishing travel commutes from Tucson, Arizona became less frequent. In the late 90's, she convinced her husband David that owning a small condo in Vancouver would be a great summer escape from the heat and she would be closer to British Columbia fishing.

I am personally familiar with many of the destinations and fishing opportunities about which Mary is writing. This is a reliable guide for information. Mary makes it a habit to be honest in her evaluations and to select fisher-friendly places closest to the best angling waters. She always looks for the most positive and best experience for the angler.

That approach is evident in her other books including *The Complete Idiot's Guide to Sharks*, *Scuba Caribbean*, and *Caribbean Sport Fishing*. Mary calls upon her expertise along with 40 years of angling experience to provide a practical and authoritative guide for anglers fishing British Columbia. This is a book that I wish I'd had time to write and this guide should be on the device of any angler who is fishing in British Colombia.

Owen Bird, Executive Director, Sport Fishing Institute of British Columbia

Introduction

In the morning's early hour, anglers gather in the South Terminal near Vancouver International Airport. Many boast fishing destination t-shirts, a few grasp new rod cases. Although many are exhausted from jetlag or late night pre-fishing partying, their excitement permeates the small building. Anglers arriving in Vancouver on inbound flights from fishing camps eagerly wait at the baggage claim.

While they are likely to be headed to Haida Gwaii, other destinations include Vancouver Island, Desolation Sound, the Inside Passage, Milbanke Sound, or interior watersheds like the Skeena, Dean, or Elk Rivers.

Each summer, hundreds of thousands of anglers pass through Richmond and Vancouver on their route to a British Columbia fishing destination. For some, it may be their first fishing journey. Others are professional guides who welcome diversity and quality, like British Columbia's "trophy-size fish." Whether they are fly fishing, trolling, or bottom fishing, they are in the Province to find fish, and plenty of fish.

Anglers arriving in Vancouver on inbound flights from fishing camps eagerly wait at the baggage claim to pick up their flash frozen boxed trophies of fresh salmon. Once they've claimed their fish, they share stories with the outgoing passengers. For those who occasionally lift their heads from the rod, the beauty and diversity of the environment is on par with the fishing. Haida Gwaii, about 50 miles southwest of

Alaska's southernmost point, offers visitors a rugged beauty and landscape of volcanic rock pinnacles with craggy shorelines lined by jagged foliage that shows the impact of years of gale-force winds. Further south, the west coast of Vancouver Island offers similar rugged views, against a backdrop of mountaintop glaciers.

Wildlife abounds throughout the region. In Haida Gwaii, bald eagles are as prolific as sparrows are in Southwest Arizona. It is not uncommon to sight a peregrine falcon or tufted puffin. Well-fed black bears scavenge beaches during low tide, mostly ignoring small-racked Sitka deer. On the mainland, anglers share their wilderness with both grizzlies and black bears, and lakes echo with the distinctive call of the loon. Passengers on inland flights often fly over small herds of Dall sheep, migrating over the glacier-draped mountains.

The pleasures of civilization, or at least those important to the serious angler, are all here. In spots from Haida Gwaii to Milbanke Sound south of Prince Rupert, from the mainland shore to Vancouver Island, visitors can eat well and heartily. Those looking for a little luxury have their choice of some of the finest upscale fishing resorts. British Columbia's fishing infrastructure is not lacking for either luxury or budget travelers. Anglers can hire personal fishing guides or tow their own boats directly to the water. There are choices for everyone.

History of Salmon Fishing

Longtime anglers can reflect on memories of Vancouver Island's Campbell River Tyee Club of British Columbia. The Club was founded in 1924 by anglers who returned to Campbell River each year in pursuit of the elusive "tyee." This 30-plus pound Chinook salmon's name translates to the Coastal First Nation meaning of "The Chief."

Campbell River's Tyee pool has a definite protocol. Anglers fish quietly in small, classic row boats. No motors are allowed. The rower will slip the boat into the currents and eddies of the pool, trolling a basic plug or spoon, one that vibrates in the current. The angler must stay focused on the action of the lure as the bite is felt in the hand as much as being seen by the bending a rod tip. That subtle bite requires that the hook must be set, both fast and hard. When a Chinook is hooked, anything can happen. If the fish is boated, and weighs 30 pounds or more, the catch is recorded and the proud angler becomes a member of the Tyee Club!

Salt and Fresh Water Species

Salmon

Being anadramous, salmon depend on both fresh and saltwater ecosystems during their life cycles.

- **Chinook or spring**—black gums with a spotted tail. The largest of the salmon species. 1.5 kg (3 lbs) to 30 kg (60 lbs)

- **Coho or Silver**—thick tail base with small spots covering tail and head. 1.3 kg (2.8 lbs) to 14 kg (30 lbs)

- **Pink**—tiny scales, large oval spots on V-shaped tail. 2.2 kg (4.8 lbs) to 5.5 kg (12 lbs)

- **Chum**—white tip on anal fin with narrow tail base. 4.5 kg (10 lbs) to 6.5 kg (14 lbs)

- **Sockeye**—almost toothless with prominent eyes. 2.2kg (4.8 lbs) to 3 kg (6.6 lbs)

- **Steelhead**—thick tail base, small spots over entire tail and head. 2.5 kg (5.5 lbs) to 10 kg (22 lbs)

Sturgeon

Elongated bodies, ranging from 7–12 feet (2-3½ m) in length, lack scales, and occasionally grow to 18 feet (5.5 m). Most sturgeons are anadromous bottom-feeders who spawn upstream and feed in river deltas, particularly the Fraser River and its estuaries.

Trout

- **Rainbow**—averaging between 0.5 kg (1lb) and 2.3 kg (5 lb), either lake-dwelling or anadromous forms may reach 9.1 kg (20 lbs). Adult fish have a lateral line from their gills to tail, which is distinguished by a broad reddish stripe. This stripe is most vivid in breeding males.

- **Cutthroat**—this popular sport fish especially appeals to fly fishers. Its name refers to a distinctive red coloration on the underside of the lower jaw.

- **Bull**—a member of the char family, its fins have white leading edges with an unusually large head and mouth. They have been measured up to 103 cm (41 in.) in length and weighing 14.5 kg (32 lb). They are either migratory, moving throughout large river systems, lakes, and the ocean, or they may remain resident.

Halibut

More elongated than most flatfishes, halibut have diamond-shaped bodies with a lateral line arching over their pectoral fin into a crescent-shaped tail. Their skin is embedded with small scales. Both eyes are located on their dark or upper sides that are used as camouflage. Coloring on the dark side varies, but is typically similar in color to the ocean bottom. Their underside is lighter, appearing more like the sky from below. This halibut adaptation enables them to avoid detection from predators. Being one of the largest flatfish, they can grow to more than 2.4 m (8 ft) and weigh as much as 230 kg (500 lbs). Significantly smaller halibut, known as "chickens", are preferable for eating. In order to conserve the larger size species, many areas have placed weight restrictions on keeping fish.

Rockfish

Thirty-six of the 100 species of rockfish can be found in British Columbia's waters. Typically caught near rocky bottoms, they are known for their longevity. One of the more popular species, frequently called a red snapper, is the yelloweye identified by its red-colored back with orange to yellow sides, and black fin tips. Lingcod, the largest of the rockfish, have been weighed up to 32 kg (70 lbs). Voracious predators, their favorite food is smaller octopus. Lingcod that survive larval stages have few predators, the exception being marine mammals like the sea lion.

(Source: *Fisheries and Oceans Canada*)

Albacore Tuna

Yes, Albacore tuna, the "white meat Charlie of the Sea," have migrated north to become an exciting sport fishing opportunity for several weeks north following the drift of warming currents during late summer. Open water or pelagic predators, these tuna have followed herring and sardines north with the trend of warming currents. Found in all tropical and temperate oceans, their migration within range of west coast fishing lodges has added a new dimension and diversity to the fish species of British Columbia.

Fishing Techniques

Mooching

Mooching is considered a traditional way to fish for Chinook. The key is to obtain bait that rolls through the water. This is achieved by cutting a perfect angle on a herring then baiting it with a tandem hook. It is theorized that the slower a herring or sardine bait rolls, the more attractive it is to larger fish. Depending on the current and depth of fish, free weights range between two and eight ounces.

Trolling

Cut plug bait, used to target all salmon species, is trolled from a downrigger to achieve greater depths. The primary advantage is the ability to increase speed and cover a greater area in less time. Many varieties of bait are used: spoons, plugs, hoochies, flashers, anchovies, and herring bait sometime covered with teaser heads. A typical trolling depth is between 20 ft (6 m) and 120 ft (36 m).

Jigging

This technique is used primarily for bottom fishing for halibut and rockfish. The bait is lowered to the ocean bottom and the jig or bait is bounced up and down. When the bite is felt, sometimes after gentle nibbling, the angler sets the hook. Heavier rods are used with level wind reels and line weights between 80 lb (36 kg) to 100 lb (45 kg) test.

Fly Fishing

Experienced anglers wanting to fly fish are most attracted to steelhead or bucktailing streamers for coho when they are plentiful and swimming on the ocean surface. During the fall when salmon enter streams to spawn, fly fishing for pinks or humpies or chum is an experience frequently shared with bears bulking up for winter hibernation by feasting on the struggling salmon trying to make their way upstream.

Fly fishing in British Columbia dates back to 1888 when James Arthurs Lees and Walter Clutterbuck explored the waters of the Upper Columbia and Kootenays. Their experience was published in *B. C. 1887 A Ramble in British Columbia.*

In recent years, spey and switch fly rods have become popular for fishing British Columbia rivers edged by temperate forest banks. The spey rod, increasingly popular as a roll-casting tool, diminishes the worry of back casting and hooking brush. Two-handed switch rods provide greater casting distance with lighter weight and longer rods requiring less shoulder effort The 2-handed switch rods provide greater distance on lighter weight and longer rods without requiring much shoulder effort.

Spin Casting

This tried and true fishing technique is seldom used for ocean fishing. It is typically an option for those interested in fishing streams who have not mastered the technique of fly fishing.

The Life Cycle of a Salmon

While there are variations in migrating and spawning habits of different species, each has a challenging odyssey, one that is difficult to imagine. If biologists are correct, a female sockeye will deposit 4,000 fertilized eggs. If 800 hatch, approximately 200 fry will survive to return to the sea where they are called smolts.

Ten of these will survive with only two returning to their spawning grounds to repeat the cycle. Others will succumb to trout and other hungry fish, birds, bears, eels, seals, before they encountered commercial and sport fishermen. They also have to deal with Mother Nature's heat, fire, and drought. The life of a salmon is a long, treacherous journey.

The life of the salmon is a fragile one.

Department of Fisheries and Oceans Canada

The Pacific Region of Fisheries and Oceans Canada, referred to as DFO, manages and protects the marine resources of Canada's west coast. This includes the province of British Columbia and its northern rivers boundaries with the Yukon Territory. This area covers more than 10,424.76 square miles (27,000 km) of coastline, 105 river systems, as well as inland salmon fisheries. The government agency is also responsible for issuing fishing licenses.

Fishing Licenses
Freshwater Fishing Licenses

All anglers are required to have a fishing license and be familiar with the policies of the type of fish and area in which they are fishing. Types of licenses vary by age and residency. They can be purchased by going to: www.env.gov.bc.ca/fw/fish/licences.

Tidal Waters Sport Fishing License

Saltwater fishing licenses have different requirements and limits determined by the area in which you are fishing. All anglers fishing for salmon must purchase a salmon stamp and record their catch. Daily limits for species vary but the maximum for Chinook are two with a total trip limit of eight.

www.pac.dfo-mpo.gc.ca/fm-gp/rec/index-eng.html

Certified Guides

The mission of the SFI CTAG Certified Tidal Angling Guide program is to establish the best standards and practices used in the sport fishing industry and guiding community. This Guide program works in partnership with relevant agencies to insure that fisheries remain sustainable and well managed. They recognize the value between tourism and sport fishing in British Columbia.

British Columbia regulates freshwater guides by requiring them to have a license. Each fishery assigns a specific number of rod days to each guide. They control the fishery by assigning rod days to guides for specific waters. Fisheries and Oceans Canada (DFO) does not license saltwater guides.

(Source: SFI CTAG Certified Tidal Angling Guide Certification and Membership Program)

Sport Fishing Institute

The Sport Fishing Institute of British Columbia is a nonprofit organization of members and contributors including: fishing lodges, resorts, certified tidal angling guides, hotels, charter operators, manufacturers, distributors, tackle shops, dealers, boat marine manufacturers, regional airlines, individual anglers and key insurance industry organizations. Their mission is to ensure the sustainability of British Columbia's natural resources by maintaining and promoting angling opportunities. The Sport Fishing Institute is supported by membership fees and contributions from anglers and the many businesses that serve and benefit from them.

(Source: The Sport Fishing Institute of British Columbia)

Pacific Salmon Foundation

British Columbia values its salmon species. The Pacific Salmon Foundation, a non-profit organization, is committed to broadening awareness and understanding about the Pacific salmon ecological, economic, and cultural values to the Province. The Foundation produces strategic communications to connect and motivate people, community organizations, businesses, and governments to protect, conserve, and rebuild wild Pacific salmon populations in British Columbia as well as the Yukon Territories and the United States Pacific Northwest.

Their principles include that Pacific salmon are invaluable to Canada's west coast cultures, economies, and ecology, as well as that maximizing diversity in salmon and their habitats is necessary to maintain and restore salmon through an uncertain future.

The Pacific Salmon Foundation must provide objective and non-partisan advice in fostering a progressive and positive attitude toward the future of Pacific salmon.

Policies and program decisions will be guided by the best available knowledge: scientific, experiential, and traditional. A fundamental role of the Pacific Salmon Foundation is to communicate widely to share knowledge about salmon and their circumstances.

Pacific Salmon Foundation must ensure transparent and accountable use of funds, fairness and objectivity in decision making, and integrity and mutual respect in all partnerships.

People are a central threat to salmon, but also the key to their sustainability. The Pacific Salmon Foundation must be inclusive of all people, and recognize the unique contributions they provide and their potential power for change.

(courtesy of Pacific Salmon Foundation)

What to Take With You

The majority of lodges and guides include fishing gear, flotation and rain suit gear, and lunch. It is important to check what is included with your fishing and be prepared for all kinds of weather including rain, rough water, and cold weather. If you are "faint of stomach", be sure to medicate for motion sickness. The key ingredient is to layer your clothing from long underwear to fleece plus gloves, boots, and a hat. Hopefully you will need sunscreen and in some destinations, mosquito repellant is a necessity.

Gateway Cities

Richmond, Vancouver, and Vancouver Island's city of Victoria are the primary gateway cities to the fishing lodges and operators throughout British Columbia.

How to Use This Guide

There are literally thousands of fishing lodges and operators throughout the Province. Featured by geographical location, the lodges included in this book range from ultra-luxurious to the more moderate, as well as destinations where anglers can hire a guide for a day of fishing rather than purchase a committed fishing package like those offered by dedicated fishing lodges. Several places are self-contained for the experienced, well-equipped angler. While there is never a guaranteed of catching or releasing fish, and while we have not visited all British Columbia operations, if we have had an unpleasant experience, we have omitted the operation.

When deciding where to fish, some of the questions to address include: the species of the fish, the size and cost of the lodge, amenities included, distance to their prime fishing grounds, type of boats and equipment included, and water conditions. Is there a lee or calm area when seas are rough?

There are thousands of places to fish in British Columbia. If there is water, ocean, rivers, or lakes, there are fish. It would be impossible to visit every lodge or fish with each independent guide. Some luxurious lodges offer much more than fishing. This book includes guides that serve areas where you might be staying in a hotel, or campground. It is incumbent on the angler to verify the current quality of lodges and guides included in this book, and verify that they are still in operation. Ask for references and inquire about the quality of fishing and species of fish prevalent during your specific time frame.

British Columbia Lodges and Fisheries

Haida Gwaii Introduction

Haida Gwaii, formerly known as Queen Charlotte Islands, is an archipelago located along the northern coast of British Columbia. The islands, separated from the mainland by Hecate Strait, consist of northern Graham Island and southerly Moresby Island. Haida Gwaii's total landmass of 3,931 sq. mi (10,180 km) includes approximately 150 smaller islands. Langara, the most popular location for fishing lodges, is noted for passing salmon migrations.

Charlotte Queen Adventures

Designed in 2001, the tugboat *Charlotte Queen* has provided anglers with comfort after a hard day of fishing. Each room varies between 1-3 beds with ensuite washrooms.

There is fresh fare served from dawn until bedtime in a lounge overlooking Nesto Inlet. Beer and wine are complimentary and mix is provided for any liquor brought. A hot breakfast buffet includes freshly baked bread, pastries, cookies, fruits, cereals, and eggs.

Food to take fishing includes a great selection of made-to-order sandwiches on freshly baked bread, cookies, fruit, and coffee. Lunch buffet is a variety of "daily specials" offering casseroles, fresh salads, or barbecue. Charlotte Queen is especially proud of their homemade soup.

In the 1990's, the *MV Charlotte Explorer* fished the west coast of what was then called the Queen Charlotte Islands, primarily exploring Englefield Bay and Hippa Island, before determining that the fishing waters around Hippa Island were the best location. In 1997, the partners of *MV Charlotte Explorer* chartered the ship in the South Pacific. Upon her return to British Columbia, they sold the ship.

Bruce Plankinton, who had fished the coastline from British Columbia to Alaska, found nothing comparable to Hippa. Bruce invested in a classic ocean-going tug. After finishing a complete first class refit to comfortably accommodate 12 guests, he rehired the former employees of the *Charlotte Explorer* to operate the ship.

When the tugboat returned to Hippa in the summer of 2001, they found the fishing better than they remembered. Bruce Plankinton feels that "Our passion was rewarded and renewed. Each season we are constantly amazed by the incredible structure that holds the bait and fish in our area. We never stop learning. It is our pleasure to share this adventure."

Dinner, usually served around 8PM, is typically a combination of meat and seafood. Robes are provided for the hot tub on the aft deck. Perfect to ease aching muscles.

Custom-made fishing boats are 18 feet long with an 8-foot beam, self-bailing with 3000 pounds of positive flotation powered by Honda 50 HP 4-stroke engines. High gunnels and a wide beam make this a stand-up, walk-around boat. Twin consoles provide each angler their own protection. Lowrance GPS units allow pinpoint accuracy to locate fish.

The boats also have sounders, VHF radios, a self-bailing fish box, and multiple rod holders.

Fishing gear provided includes 10 ½ Daiwa Mooching rods, Daiwa M-1 mooching reels, and Shimano TR 200 G level wind reels with Maxima 25-pound ultra-green line. Halibut gear is a 7-foot Berkley Rough Neck rod with Shimano TLD 20 reels.

Fishing is self-guided with an available fish master always provided. Charlotte Queen has turnover twice-weekly using Pacific Coastal Beechcraft 1900 charters to Sandspit. Anglers then fly a scenic Helijet flight to the lodge.
(Source: Charlotte Queen Adventures)
www.charlottequeenadventures.com

Langara Fishing Adventures

Langara Fishing Adventures began as a discussion of a group of angling friends who were looking for a better place to fish. Between the 1970's and 80's, British Columbia's Campbell River and River's Inlet were the best known destinations for salmon fishing. In those days, the remoteness of the Queen Charlotte Islands (now Haida Gwaii) was unknown to the well-traveled angler. Its isolated location kept it undiscovered by the sport fishing community, but rumors spread that its fishery was more abundant than any other on the British Columbia's west coast.

Fueled by an adventurous spirit, Rick Bourne and his friends made plans to venture north to these remote waters. They decided to take a chance on a small island named Langara.

Sport fishing at Langara Island began in 1985, when Bourne and three Noble brothers towed a renovated 120-foot paddle wheeler to Langara Island, anchored it in a protective cove, and set out to discover the island's secrets.

They explored Parry Pass on windy days using a 14-foot fiberglass boat with a 15-hp motor. There were no fishing tips or GPS-marked favorite halibut holes.

Conversations about the abundance of fish caught at Langara Island quickly filled their lodge with anglers, and each season brought further expansion of their operations. Word also spread about the island's pristine environment and diversity of wildlife, attracting adventure travelers to share the experience with avid anglers.

Langara Fishing Adventures' five remote lodges showcase some of the very best of British Columbia's diverse wilderness, wildlife, and sport fishing opportunities, ranging from world famous salmon and halibut off Langara Island to hard-fighting steelhead in the quiet rivers of Haida Gwaii, as well as fly fishing for wild rainbow trout in the Chilcotin wilderness.

Chinook Lodge

Chinook Lodge features a towering river-rock fireplace and a spacious main lounge and dining table for sharing the day's fish tales. The Lodge accommodates up to 22 guests in well-appointed double occupancy rooms.

Eagle Lodge

The most luxurious accommodation located on the grounds of Langara Island Lodge offers a more intimate experience with six suites, a fully staffed kitchen, game room, and a "top of the island" view. It is an ideal venue for couples or corporate groups.

Raven Cottage

Secluded in the ancient forest, Raven Cottage is available for small groups wanting to enjoy their adventure on Langara in ultimate privacy.

Alaska View Lodge

Located along the north coast of Graham Island, between Masset and Tow Hill. Alaska View Lodge is surrounded by the ancient rainforest of Naikoon Park on the beach overlooking Dixon Entrance and the distant Alaskan Islands.

The main house can accommodate 12 anglers in six double-occupancy rooms. There is a common lounge, spacious sundeck, outdoor hot tub, and satellite television. Adjacent to the main lodge is a 2-bedroom guesthouse featuring ensuite bathrooms and a private patio. Full breakfast service is included; lunch and dinner service can be arranged.

Private Cottage Rentals

Alaska View Lodge also offers private self-serve accommodations in two nearby beachside cottages, featuring two or three bedrooms with full kitchen facilities. Single night, weekly, and monthly rentals can be arranged. For reservations call the lodge directly at 1.800.661.0019 or info@alaskaviewlodge.ca.

Kumdis River Lodge

This quiet wilderness setting is located between Masset Inlet and the Kumdis River. The well-appointed main cabin provides accommodations for eight guests in four bedrooms. The cabin features a common dining and living area, fireplace, satellite TV, an outdoor hot tub, and a gazebo.

For tourists visiting the Islands, Kumdis River Lodge is centrally located near Port Clements on Graham Island, just off the main Island road. It is available for full service accommodations, including fine dining, or as a simple cottage rental. All meals, and alcohol with meals, are included in our guided fishing packages.

Moosehead Lodge

Located in British Columbia's interior Chilcotin region, this rustic lakeside lodge is surrounded on all sides by rugged wilderness and is accessible only by floatplane. The area offers a truly world class fishing experience for avid fly anglers and is a great retreat for small groups and families with children of all ages.

The Chilcotin provides access to numerous lakes and rivers throughout the region, including the blue ribbon fishing of the Blackwater and Upper Dean rivers.

A Mary L. Peachin Adventure

Eagles outnumber Heermann's sea gulls dive-bombing bait balls of schooling frenzied herring feasting on plankton krill. Nearby humpback whales breech and fin as if waving to busy salmon anglers who barely have time to take notice of the cetaceans. Someone radios that three black bears are grubbing for food in Bruin Bay. For the serious angler, the rugged island of Langara is as close as it gets to the heavenly fishing kingdom in Haida Gwaii.

"You should have been here yesterday (...when the fishing was really great)." Yes, all anglers know that fishing story. But this one is different. Mark McAneeley was guiding anglers when 40-some killer whales (orcas) surfaced. Suddenly the pod divided and 10 of these magnificent creatures, frolicking and blowing bubbles, circled Mark's boat. Their intention was to eat a fighting hooked salmon, but they took their time. After 10 minutes, they suddenly grabbed the fish and sounded, leaving the amazed angler with a straightened hook.

Fortunately, these orcas were a migrating pod. When these voracious hunters pass through a fishery, they devour both salmon and bait. Fish that escape head for the unknown. It may have been an awesome sight, but it made for a slower day of fishing for the arriving 28 guests at Langara's Island Lodge.

Located 200-feet on top of a hillside of old growth forest, the cedar lodge, the smaller and most luxurious of Langara's fishing lodges, overlooks wind-protected Henslung Cove. An 8-person ski hill-type tram carries guests between the dock and the lodge. River otters swim beneath the dock, playfully welcoming newcomers.

Not a moment is wasted. Brunch is ready for arriving anglers and with satiated appetites; they head to the fishing grounds. The boats are 25-foot custom-made Ironwood aluminum boats with two 90-hp 4-stroke engines. It's a 15-minute motor to speed anglers to the popular fishing grounds of Cohoe Point. The stable boats have high transoms providing greater rod leverage while fishing. A compact, flushing head, so convenient for women, is located under the center console.

Guide Mark McAneeley with Chinook, photo credit Mary L. Peachin

Several dozen boats mooch (trolling slowly with weighted lines using barbless hooks with cut-plugged herring bait) the protected cove because high northwest winds churning the surf do not permit venturing further west along the rocky coastline.

Minutes after lowering the lines 17 pulls or about 35 feet, a small 20-ish pound Chinook (spring) nibbles. Waiting patiently while feeling the bite, Mark watches the rod bend then says "hook it." 20 pounders were small with five tyees caught including a 52-pound release and a 65-pound trophy.

Wearing a toque over his fishing cap for warmth and surgical latex gloves to protect against the salty brine of the herring bait, Mark is an experienced guide requested by anglers from all over the world.

Unlike many other guides, the ones at Langara don't hook biting fish for the guests. Hooking any fish is the challenge and fun part of the angling experience and, here, the novice has the opportunity to learn. Single-action Islander reels (rather than the easier level-wind type) with lighter 20-pound test line adds more sport than the method of down rigging at deeper depths, used by many fishing operations.

Mooching requires more skill for the angler to hook the fish and the guide has to determine the depth where the fish are hanging out and feeding. If the angler doesn't anticipate the run of the fish during the fight, well, the handles of the reel are called "knuckle-busters" for a good reason.

There wasn't much time lapse between fish and another Chinook on the line followed by a jumper who was successful in unhooking himself. When the fishing slacked off, we had time to admire bald eagles fishing. When herring splashed in the water like raindrops on a windshield, Mark caught them on bare hooks to use as tomorrow's bait, because "they have to be stiff with rigor mortis to spin through the water correctly, so I catch them today to fish with tomorrow."

As Mark described it, we were fishing in the "last frontier." These salmon grounds are as far north as you can fish in British Columbia. On a clear day you can see the southeast panhandle of Alaska. In Mark's estimation, there isn't a better place for salmon and halibut fishing.

Before quitting time at 7:30pm, we stopped on our return to the Lodge for a few minutes fishing in Bruin Cove. We were hoping to see a black or grizzly bear, but this is also the spot where the sizable salmon hang out. A red-footed pigeon guillemot swam by the boat, robin-like marbled murrelet dove quickly, and brown white-bellied rhinoceros auklet dived for herring.

Langara is not for "fair weather anglers or the faint of stomach." Gale force wind (+30mph) can whip the ocean swell as high as 30 feet. Leaving the protection of Cohoe Point or McPherson to fish favorites like Andrews Point or the island's west coast Lighthouse and No Name Point requires a calmer day.

Don't tell that to Helen Hennekam, an octogenarian from Vancouver. In the early part of the 5-day trip, she landed the biggest Chinook of the week, a 36-1/2 pound tyee. Later in the week Peter Cliromos of Vancouver caught a 65-pound trophy fish and Paul Bauer of Long Island released a 52-pounder. While bottom fishing, Richard Bailey of Calgary caught a 92-pound halibut.

In Solide Passage, along Lucy Island and the route to the fishing grounds, a young humpback played in 24 feet of water. The barometer was rising and so were the salmon. Now able to navigate the waters to reach McPherson and Andrews Points, we had access to different salmon fishing grounds. Another day when the wind shifted, we headed southeast passing Cox Island stopping to search for bright-beaked puffin nesting on cliffs. The island is unusual with interesting rock formations and a hole in rock.

Changing winds also allowed us to fish southeast in the open ocean on the western coast near Lacy Island and the Lighthouse. We didn't have time to watch the Heerman and Herring gulls and bald eagles feeding or another humpback finning and breeching. Our time was spent enjoying 10 consecutive double hookups, fighting Chinook ranging from 20-30 pounds for three solid hours.

Aching biceps cried for ibuprofen and a soak in one of the lodge's two hot tubs. Stripping off the bright red survivor suits worn by all anglers, the warm water was perfect even in the rain. On the hillside, Sitka black tail deer nibbled the grass like lawnmowers.

The island of Langara is uninhabited except for 4 fishing lodges and a remote lighthouse on the northwest side of the island. This beacon, built in 1907, is illuminated by a 500-watt bulb. The lighthouse, manned by a couple, is the first sighting of land seen by ships visiting North America. The rough waters along this portion of the rugged coast frequently make the trip by boat impossible. The red-topped lighthouse beacon is accessible by helicopter and our A-Star 6-

passenger helicopter landed in the front yard.

Five of us were given a tour of the lighthouse, including its tsunami reader, then welcomed into the home where we were served spiced ice tea and blueberry cake. Before returning across the trail-less island, we landed briefly on the white sandy beach of Lepas Bay.

Thirty years ago, Vancouver schoolteacher Rick Bourne and his partners, the Noble brothers, lived their dream. In 1984, they became aware of some great salmon fishing statistics from commercial operators around Langara. Rick sold his charter boat, and he, Richard, Robert, and John Noble started a small fishing lodge. They brought in a floating barge, which they converted to a lodge.

Ten years later, they built the upscale (complete with Aveeda amenities in the bathrooms) 28-guest Island Lodge. Little did Bourne know that his small floating lodge for just 24 guests would become one of the most popular salmon fishing lodges in North America.

He soon expanded the Fishing Lodge to hold 50 guests and added the 200-foot tram to carry guests up and down the hillside. Today, despite some rough weather and seas, four or five day trips allow as much fishing as the guest can handle. While the fishermen play, the staff at the lodge busily rescues a newborn sea lion, umbilical cord still attached. It's just another day in the Haida Gwaii, one of salmon fishing's "last frontiers."

Maude Island Retreat

Maude Island Retreat is secluded in the Skidegate Inlet. The waterfront lodge, which accommodates up to eight people, offers the comforts of home. After a fishing day, the angler can relax in the hot tub or stretch out near the river rock fireplace.

Considered by many locals as a prime location to for discovering Haida Gwaii's pristine beauty, Maude Island Retreat is a 17.5 acre homestead which includes a comfortable lounging area, spacious dining room, wide open patio, large stone fire pit, and a hot tub.

Generous home-style meals are served with daily housekeeping service provided. Gameday and Knotty Girl are 28-foot welded-aluminum boat powered with by a 300 horsepower, 4-stroke Mercury engine. The two fishing boats have a head on board, the best electronics, and can fish up to four downriggers at a time.

Maude Island Retreat's fully guide fishing package includes: water taxi transport from Sandspit to Maude Island Retreat with an option to upgrade to a helicopter, all meals and complimentary beer and wine, four nights of accommodation based on double occupancy, professional guiding, 10 hours daily of fishing, rain gear and boots, vacuum packaging for catch, and an available hot tub and card room available.

(Source: Maude Island Retreat)

www.maudeisland.com

Naden Lodge

Located in the village of Masset on the northern coast of Graham Island, the cedar post and beam resort lodge has a waterfront view of the harbor.

Its newly renovated amenities include non-smoking rooms, high-speed internet, a pool table, satellite television, spacious sitting room, large sundeck, and an outdoor hot tub. There is also a dry room and a gift shop. Anglers can watch the guides expertly clean and prepare their catch at the dockside fish weigh and cleaning station.

The renovations have included rebuilding and enlarging the Lodge deck, better seating, and outdoor patio heaters. A new master harbor-view bedroom has been added. The lodge now includes six bedrooms with a capacity for 13 anglers. Naden Lodge now offers private rooms as well as those with queen-sized beds for couples.

Naden Lodge is located in the middle of the salmons' migratory route to their spawning streams. Whether salmon are headed to major river systems of mainland British Columbia, the west coast of the United States, or a multitude of salmon streams along the west coast of Vancouver Island, these fish must first pass the Haida Gwaii (formerly Queen Charlotte Islands).

Just minutes across Masset Inlet, Eagles Nest is Naden's first halibut and salmon fishing spot. Other proven fishing hot spots include: The Green Can, Hidden Island, Wiah Point, Cape Edenshaw, Bird Rock, and Shag Rock, to name a few. Experienced guides know historical migrations and when and where to troll a line.

Naden Lodge ocean fishing is fully guided for either beginners or the experienced. They are happy to show an angler how to use a downrigger, set up bait, and teach downrigger fishing, trolling or cut plugging. Each day, they make the effort to fish both slack tide changes. At Naden Lodge they try to ensure every comfort to anglers. They value boat comfort and fish in five Boston Whaler Conquest 255's. These boats have rain covers and on-board washroom facilities.

Equipped with quality electronics and stocked with the best of fishing gear, Islander reels are included. The boats have running fresh water, raw water wash down, fish storage, twin Scotty electric downriggers, and deep water halibut rods. Processing is done in Masset's local cannery. Each boat is also outfitted with high quality GPS and fish finder combo units, VHF radio, and Sirius Satellite Radio.

Another advantage of visiting Naden Lodge is that their private aircraft includes a charter from Calgary and other British Columbia gateways including Red Deer, Edmonton, Grande Prairie, Kelowna, Kamloops, Prince George and others.

(Source: Naden Lodge)

www.nadenlodge.com

Peregrine Lodge

Peregrine Lodge's land based resort includes a two story post and beam main lodge with large windows and decks providing panoramic views of Naden Harbour

A central fireplace is surrounded by leather couches and chairs, giving guests a place to tell fish tales after a long day. An upstairs library is an option to sit back and relax. Bear, Raven, and Eagle cabins, adjacent to the main house, have 11 single rooms. Cabins #4, 5, and 6, surrounding a pitch and putt course, have four bedrooms. A robe and slippers are included.

Three new guesthouses have 4-bedroom private accommodations with ensuite bathrooms. Guest rooms are serviced daily and amenities include robe and slippers.

Bring a hearty appetite. The chef takes pride in preparing gourmet entrees with delectable appetizers that include fresh Dungeness crab. All produce is flown in fresh to ensure the finest quality and selection.

An expanded sports lounge offers a fitness room with a view, a quiet television and a card room to play either pool or poker. Peregrine

Lodge has a secluded hot tub with a massage facility. Golfers can practice their skills on a 9-hole pitch and putt course.

Fully guided saltwater fishing packages for salmon and halibut include 10 1/2 hours per day excluding departure day in Peregrine's fleet of 17-foot Boston Whalers. Guests wanting to upgrade to a larger boat, with on board washroom facilities, can select either a 23-foot Edgewater or a 24-foot Bayliner Trophy.

All anglers are provided with a full complement of fishing equipment and specialized outerwear for comfort and protection on the water. Trolling a cut-plug herring is the standard method for enticing the salmon species, while halibut are typically taken by jigging bait off the bottom.

Guests may choose to travel to the fishing grounds in the custom-built 30 foot, 12-passenger "Peregrine One." The boat remains at the fishing grounds, located approximately 45 minutes from the Lodge, which offers added comfort and safety, monitoring weather, and a washroom facility.

Experienced guides will navigate fully equipped boats, assist with tackle, gear and bait, and clean and prepare your catch. Peregrine's fishing grounds are ideally located in the path of mature salmon as they travel to spawning rivers.

A freshwater experience is available on secluded Eden Lake in a large pontoon boat. Other activities include kayaking, and heli-tours or fishing.

(Source Peregrine Lodge)

www.peregrinelodge.com

Queen Charlotte Lodge

Built in 1991, Queen Charlotte Lodge has offered comfortable accommodations in a warm atmosphere with genuine hospitality. The lodge pole pine lodge overlooks Naden Harbour where at sunset from friends can gather to swap fish tales on the waterfront deck or near a crackling fire in the great stone hearth. Look forward to the fantastic welcome barbeque that kicks off the first night of your stay.

While the lodge's 24 waterfront guest rooms are the perfect place to get away from it all, there is still the option to stay connected via state-of-the-art satellite communications and Wi-Fi network.

The 12 upstairs rooms are configured with a queen and twin bed; main floor rooms are suited for triple occupancy with three twin beds. All rooms feature private ensuite facilities.

Charlotte House

A short boardwalk stroll from the Main Lodge, Charlotte House's six double-occupancy bedrooms with four bathrooms are comfortably appointed and can be configured to suit the needs of your group.

Since its construction in 1992, Charlotte House has consistently been in demand by groups returning for their annual fishing retreat. With its own hot tub gazebo and build-to-your-specs bar service, Charlotte House offers exclusive features that will ensure your fishing vacation is everything you could want it to be.

Haida House

This chalet enjoys its own private space on the lodge property just yards from the beach. Its front deck hot tub is a great place to kick back after a day of fishing.

The cedar-clad house accommodates eight guests in three upstairs bedrooms and one on the main level, furnished in twin and bunk-style bed configurations. Haida House offers a kitchen, dining area, living room with three shared bathrooms. Amenities include a fireplace, leather furniture, and satellite television.

Totem House

The newest accommodation is a log chalet at the water's edge. Four suites with two queen beds and ensuite baths occupy the top level of this chalet. Each room features an inside and outside entrance as well as beautifully finished ensuite washrooms.

Other amenities include a flat panel satellite television, digital phone service, and Wi-Fi connection. A private chef and hostess provide exclusive tailor-made bar and dining services in the Totem House's private lounge and dining room. Totem House also offers a lower lounge providing guests a multi-use space suitable for meeting and group events. On the lower level, a multimedia boardroom and an executive workout facility, complimented by spa and massage rooms, complete the Totem House package.

MV Driftwood

The Driftwood serves as Queen Charlotte Lodge's operations center on its fishing grounds. It's also a great place to take a break during the fishing day to enjoy a full lunch service.

Anchored in quiet water on the fishing grounds, the Driftwood serves as a hub for the diehard fisherman. For those who want to maximize their fishing time, the vessel can accommodate up to 12 guests aboard. A private chef and crew pampering make this an ideal accommodation for keen anglers.

Queen Charlotte Lodge fly chartered aircraft, an Air North Boeing 737-200, for the 1.5-hour flight from Vancouver's South Terminal to Masset. The flight to the lodge is a short 15-minute scenic ride on a 12-passenger Sikorsky S-76 helicopter.

(Source: Queen Charlotte Lodge)
www.queencharlottelodge.com

The West Coast Fishing Club

In the summer of 1981, businessman Rick Grange, an avid salmon angler, explored British Columbia's northern west coast. Overwhelmed by the pristine beauty of the coast's marine wilderness along with its superlative (as in a double hookup of two 50+pound) salmon fishing, the following summer, he invited business partner Brian Legge to explore with him.

The men purchased two Boston Whalers, hired some experienced guides, and blocked rooms at a Graham Island lodge to host additional guests. By 1988, the beginning of what would become The West Coast Fishing Club (WCFC) was established. At that time the area was considered a part of the Queen Charlotte Islands. In 2010, the Island's name was officially changed to Haida Gwaii, which translates to "islands of the people."

View of Parry Passage, photo credit Mary L. Peachin

The two conservation-minded men concluded that there had to be a better choice for accommodating guests. They decided to construct a land-based lodge. The following year, after acquiring North Island Lodge in Beal Cove on the lee side of Langara Island, they purchased a barge.

They renovated it to offer high quality, rustic, yet elegant accommodations. In the summer of 1990, North Island Lodge, located at the northernmost point in the Queen Charlottes, opened.

At the same time, ground was broken in Henslung Cove for what would become The Clubhouse. By 1991, to complement some of the world's best ocean fishing, anglers were welcomed to luxury wilderness accommodations and excellent cuisine paired with fine wine. The West Coast Fishing Club (WCFC) experience was further enhanced by chartering guests to the Clubhouse in helicopters after their chartered flight arrival from Vancouver into the Masset airport.

In the summer of 2001, they opened The Outpost, a third and even more exclusive, luxurious lodge along the coastline of Graham Island. Located on the farthest western edge of Haida Gwaii, it is the most remote fishing lodge in the region. Surrounded by untouched wilderness, guests found tranquility in this private, luxury oasis along with prolific runs of salmon, halibut, and other ocean species.

The West Coast Fishing Club opened their headquarters just steps away from Vancouver International Airport's South Terminal. The proximity to charter flights enabled staff to welcome guests on their outbound and return flights.

Almost two decades later, The West Coast Fishing Club offers anglers three accommodation options. Located offshore Port Louis of Graham Island, the largest and most western of Haida Gwaii's two main islands is The Outpost. The Club's most remote property is one of private luxury for 14 anglers. Fishing in the open ocean, there are prolific salmon runs as well as deep-water fishing for halibut and rockfish.

The Outpost's unique surroundings might tempt an angler away from fishing in their 22-foot Boston Whalers. There is the opportunity to kayak, beachcomb remote and isolated beaches, or a hike in the coastal rainforest. Whale watching is at its best at this location, with species including orca, gray, humpbacks, and the occasional blue and minke whales.

While this may be a remote wilderness experience, its accommodations are as luxurious as staying in a Vancouver upscale hotel. Appointed with rich leather furnishings, a large stone fireplace, a billiard table, and satellite access, the lounge area is overwhelming with its panoramic ocean views. A simple step onto the deck offers tired muscles an opportunity to relax in a hot tub sharing the view. The Outpost chefs delight in pairing delectable entrées, featuring local seafood with British Colombia wines.

The original floating lodge, North Island Lodge, offers a total of 12 single- or double-occupancy rooms, each with an ensuite bathroom and amenities including plush bath robes and towels, shampoo, conditioner, moisturizer, soap and turndown service. Comfy beds have down duvets and pillows with high-thread count linens.

Ideally located on a channel to prime fishing grounds, North Island Lodge has sweeping views of Parry Pass and Lucy Island. Anglers preferring more than viewing the sunset over Haida Gwaii can enjoy their favorite sporting event on a high definition large screen satellite television.

Mealtime is always a highlight at North Island Lodge. No one leaves the table hungry with meat, poultry, and healthy options including fresh specialty. In the mornings, anglers can indulge with a "care package" of delicious pastry. and organic greens grown right in the Haida Gwaii.

North Island Lodge offers anglers the opportunity to self- or fully-guide 19- to 21-foot Eaglecraft boats fully equipped with top of the line gear.

The West Coast Fishing Club's most iconic lodge is The Clubhouse. Larger than the other lodges, it offers luxurious accommodations for 42 anglers.

Internationally trained chefs take food seriously at The Clubhouse. In the solarium-styled dining room overlooking Parry Pass, gourmet creativity is paired with an evening wine. Like their other lodges, menus feature local seafood, premium meats, and fresh organic Haida Gwaii produce. An elegant private dining room is available for groups up to 14 guests.

The Clubhouse tastefully blends 5-star luxury and service with a warm and welcoming fishing lodge design. Each well-appointed room, offering an ocean or forest view, features comfortable beds, down duvets, and private ensuites, several with Jacuzzi tubs.

Two spacious lounges are available on each of the two floors to share a drink, play pool, or enjoy a large screen satellite television. Other amenities include a spa with a massage therapist, a steam room, fitness facility, two hot tubs, a library, and, if necessary, a business center complete with Internet and quiet surrounding to conduct private calls.

Functionality, versatility, and luxury are featured in The Clubhouse fleet of 22-29-foot Boston Whalers with 200 HP Mercury engines. While self-guiding is available, most guests opt to fish with The Clubhouse's experienced certified guides. The finest fishing gear is provided, food is delivered by zodiac or "Candy Boat" mid-morning and afternoon for those still hungry or for those who have already gobbled their self-helping from the pantry's cookies, candy, sandwiches, beer, and soft drinks next to the drying room where rain suits and boots are provided.

The most decadent of any fishing weekend is Chef David Hawksworth & Friends Culinary Adventure. Joining Hawksworth, of culinary fame in Vancouver and across Canada, are several chefs who provide a weekend of the finest Northwest cuisine, between fishing and massage therapy. This has been a sold-out weekend since 2007.

A Mary L. Peachin Adventure

David Hawksworth and Friends Culinary Adventure

Fine cuisine with wine pairs well set on an exquisite island, where on a fair day you can view Alaska. When you aren't being driven down to the dock in a Hummer H1 Alpha to salmon fish in a Boston Whaler, life is four days of decadence.

It's 5:30 in the morning. Slack tide has priority over the sunrise; that's when Haida Gwaii's trophy Chinook bite. This culinary adventure is more than four days of fishing and eating. There is time for a daily massage, 2-hour cooking classes, fishing the afternoon tide, learning martini mixology, or taking a helicopter ride to explore the red striped lighthouse, rugged landscape, and uninhabited beaches of Langara Island.

Evolving from a cocktail conversation with David Hawksworth, Canada's former Chef of the Year, West Coast Exec Brian Grange "wanted to create a special weekend, one that combined a love for fishing with fine Pacific Northwest cuisine in our remote lodge wilderness setting." A culinary fishing adventure was born.
(Article featured in Robb Report)

In the summer of 2007, to enhance the company's efforts toward corporate responsibility, The West Coast Fishing Club initiated an annual Fishing for Kids tournament to raise money for BC children's charities. Holy screamin' knuckle busters! The eighth (2014) annual Fishing for Kids tournament raised a record-breaking $1,173,000 for Canucks Autism Network (CAN), surpassing last year's million-dollar mark. The winner of the 3-day event garnered a whopping $200,000 grand prize. Since 2007, the annual event has generated over $5 million for BC children's charities.

The West Coast Fishing Club, located in British Columbia's Haida Gwaii is just a 2-hour flight and too short helicopter ride to an island, isolated 50 miles south of Alaska. All West Coast Fishing Club properties, one of British Columbia's largest salmon fishing operations, has one thing in common: convenient proximity to some of the world's best ocean fishing

A Mary Peachin Adventure

Double, double, eagle! Say what? We aren't talking golf here. This is West Coast Fishing Club sport fishing on British Columbia's northernmost island, Langara, in Haida Gwaii (formerly the Queen Charlotte Islands).

My buddy Tucsonan Lori Mackstaller and I were fishing for Chinook (king or spring) salmon in a 22-foot Boston Whaler. Wham! Each of us got a hook up. The chaos, which typically ensues with a double hook up as we followed our fish around the center console to keep lines untangled, ended abruptly. A 2-ton sea lion grabbed my fish leaving only its head before grabbing Lori's fish. A bald eagle swooped down to fetch my remaining salmon head. This was a close up view of the wilderness food chain.

We were so busy that when a radio announcement was broadcasted, there wasn't time to reel in the fishing lines for a short motor to view a pod of 20 orcas swimming through Parry Passage between Lucy and Graham Island.

Lori Mackstaller with Brent Maracle holding Chinook Photo credit Mary L. Peachin

Luckily for us, those orcas swam by us after cruising through Parry Passage to the lee side of island where we were fishing. The bull, boasting a super-size dorsal fin, and his mate swam some distance from the rest of the pod. During our four days of fishing, we would also observe several solo humpbacks.

Monkey Puke and Betsy "dummy" flashers were tied to the boat, not the line. When I told Brent Maracle that I wanted to hook my own fish, he replied, "At West Coast Fishing Club, all anglers hook their own fish." How unique and refreshing not to have a guide hand over a rod with a hooked fish.

Fortune stayed with us. The sun was shining and the sea was calm. We headed to the west side to Langara's Lacy Island. Not in the lee of the island, the water and wind here can be real stomach churners. And that is more typical of weather conditions in Langara.

At one of our fine cuisine dinners, Lori and I had the opportunity to dine with Fred Schuerenberg from Missouri's boot-heel town of Sikeston. A widower, Fred was "bonding" with his new stepson over the Father's Day weekend. He didn't bother to mention that he had just caught a potential season record-breaker 60.5 pound Chinook. When a seal lion chased his fish, Fred free-spooled the line while his guide hurriedly attached the line to another rod. Sea lions can't swim as fast as salmon.

An hour later, Fred measured and photographed the fish for the record book before releasing this granddaddy. When I asked Fred why he didn't share this amazing story, he humbly told me, "I didn't want to sound boastful. This may be my first and last tyee." It wasn't and he caught another Chinook over that tyee 30-pound requirement.

Guide Brent used cut plug herring for bait. West Coast uses the finest fishing gear: Islander single-action "knuckle-busting" reels and Shimano rods. Knuckle-busting? If you don't get your hands off the reel when the salmon runs, the spinning action of the reel on your fingers is going to cause a world of hurt.

For three full days and two half days, Lori and I released salmon while fishing Lacy and the calmer lee waters of Cohoe and Andrews Point. We enjoyed the wildlife, including pigeon guillemot, numerous bald eagles, and beautiful landscapes off Seath Point and Killer Bay. There were remote, uninhabited beaches and pinnacles including Langara's iconic Flower Pot and Pillar rocks. We were transfixed by the bull kelp, white-sided dolphin, and numerous jellyfish.

British Columbia's Department of Fisheries has set some new limits on daily catches and keeping fish that West Coast flash freezes and packages for their guests. Before we hit day three, we had limited out on salmon—the only choice left was halibut fishing.

Let's be honest. Halibut are some of the best tasting fish, but they aren't a lot of fun to catch. Then again, some folks may enjoy hauling what feels like a dead weight 200 feet to the surface. Not me. We were grateful that we caught "chickens", the smaller and best tasting of the halibut.

After heading past Egeria and Dibrell Bays, we motored for about six miles. The combination of smelling herring and salmon bellies from two other boats, one anchored, attracted the halibut.

As we returned to Beal Cove, which the Clubhouse overlooks, a humpback exploded out of the water. Following his breech, he started finning. It was as if he was waving to say "so long." It may have been the completion of our fishing journey, but not the memories. www.westcoastfishingclub.com

Westcoast Fishing Resorts

Westcoast Fishing Resorts have two operations located in Haida Gwaii with the third at Milbanke Sound along British Columbia's central coast. They offer private chartered airfare to its lodge. The deluxe accommodation is all-inclusive with gourmet meals and all beverages. They offer unlimited fishing from dawn until dusk with all boats, gear, and bait provided. Fishing can be either guided or unguided.

The Resorts have a simple dining philosophy: use the finest ingredients available and prepare with care. The rest takes care of itself. They feel that their galleys are there for the angler's relaxation and enjoyment with friends.

Breakfast includes a variety of continental items as well as a hot breakfast buffet. Anglers wishing a more leisurely approach to the fishing day can take time for daily specials as well as eggs any style. A table full of goodies awaits the angler to pack for the boat along with sandwiches, soda, or beer.

Lunch is a hot buffet featuring a menu of burgers and fish and chips and a full line up of fresh salads, soups, and other items. If the salmon bite is just too good to make the trip back to the lodge, they offer hot lunch on the water as well.

Dinner is the time to relax and share the day's stories (and lies) accompanied by some of the Pacific Northwest's finest offerings both in food and drink. The 3-course service is served with complementary wine. Aperitifs and coffee accompany the Pastry Chef's nightly creations.

Westcoast Resort's Fishing Instructor Program has been designed for all ages and skill levels. A comprehensive orientation session allows even the most novice angler to quickly become familiar with safe vessel operation. Their boats' safety and navigational equipment have the quality, if necessary, to withstand the rigors of their remote locations.

Friendly and experienced WCR guides instruct guests on local fishing techniques and the lodge's current "hot spots". All fishing and premium foul-weather gear is provided; guests may also choose to bring along their own favorite rods and reels.

All packages include five hours of guided fishing instruction with the option to upgrade to a guide for 10 hours per day if booked in advance. Anglers may also opt to fish entirely on their own. This option limits allowable time on the water to daylight hours, as Westcoast Resort's commitment is to provide a safe, supervised on-water experience.

Any catch brought to the deck will be prepared by the skilled dock crew who will take fillet, vacuum pack, and flash freeze your fish. Additional options include custom fish processing: canned, smoked, or candied.

The Lodge at Hippa Island

Westcoast Fishing Lodges operate lodges at Hippa Island and Englefield Bay in Haida Gwaii as well as Milbanke Sound located along the Central Coast. Each lodge is all-inclusive, providing boats, guides, and fishing tackle. Their food is excellent, and the lodges include hot tubs and game rooms.

The Lodge at Hippa Island, considered their flagship, is located in a secluded inlet on the west side of Graham Island. The area is pristine, untapped, and boasts of some of Haida Gwaii's best fishing with large runs of migrating salmon and halibut, all in close proximity to the 24 room lodge.

(courtesy of Westcoast Fishing Resorts)

The adventure begins in Sikorsky helicopter after landing on a private float at the resort's doorstep. The area is rugged wilderness beauty with incredible cuisine.

Englefield Bay

(courtesy of Westcoast Fishing Resorts)

Established in 1995, Westcoast Resorts, Hippa, Englefield, and Milbanke, offer anglers the finest in destinations ranging from Haida Gwaii to British Columbia central coast. The location of their fishing lodges is defined by three concepts: exclusivity, remoteness, and proximity to some of the most productive salmon and halibut fishing grounds.

Their unparalleled service and amenities are all-inclusive deluxe accommodations: gourmet meals and select beverages, unlimited daylight fishing, chartered transportation, and boats, gear, and bait.

Along the west side of Moresby Island, Westcoast Fishing Lodge at Englefield Bay, which accommodates 46 guests, is known for its production of trophy-sized tyee during their short run to the area's most popular salmon and halibut fishing grounds.

The ruggedly beautiful fishing region is ideal for anglers who enjoy targeting multiple species as well as viewing interesting wildlife watching: humpbacks, pigeon guillemot, eagles, thin-billed murre, and stellar sea lions. Englefield is the perfect way to experience all that Haida Gwaii has to offer in one place.

Englefield Bay, considered the most protected fishery on the west side of Haida Gwaii, is a location passed by all of British Columbia migrating salmon species. Halibut, ling cod, and yellow eyes, also called red snapper, are available. Herring remains the bait of choice, more specifically rigged as either a cut-plug or left whole. Denham Bay and Cape Henry are fishing sites which allow anglers to fish underwater structure or tight against the kelp.

www.westcoastresorts.com

Central and Northern British Columbia

Introduction

For the purpose of this book, *Sport Fishing in British Columbia*, Central British Columbia will be defined as the area south of Prince Rupert and north of the Lower Mainland, which comprises most of Richmond and Vancouver. There are several lodges that are located north of Prince Rupert almost to the Alaska Panhandle. Areas that attract fly fishers including rivers like the Skeena, Dean, and Fraser will be focused in a separate chapter.

Central Coast Adventures

Located on Denny Island in Shearwater along British Columbia's west coast, Central Coast Adventures is approximately 300 miles (500 km) north of Vancouver. This central location allows them to offer fishing at a variety of locations including Seaforth Channel, Milbanke Sound, Hakai Pass, St Johns, Cultus Sound, Calvert Island, Ocean Falls, Namu, and more.

Fishing from 23-foot Grady White Gulfstreams, powered by twin 4-stroke 150 horsepower Yamaha outboards, Central Coast Adventures considers these boats provide stabile, safe, and protected from weather. They come equipped with Scotty electric downriggers, GPS, radar, fish finder, satellite radio, and washroom facilities. Their fleet also contains a 28-foot King Fisher Offshore for additional weather protection. The boat is warm, smooth riding, with a head for extra privacy. Their 29-foot Grady White 290 Chesapeake is powered by twin 250 horsepower Yamaha engines.

Pristine oceanfront 12-guest lodge accommodations come equipped with amenities. After waking up and eating a scrumptious breakfast, it's a simple walk down the boat ramp. Anglers can choose from private rooms located in the main lodge, or reserve our self-contained guest cabin. At the lodge, guests can enjoy a hot tub and relax for the evening after a day of fighting fish.

There are a number of services in Shearwater, including a pub, restaurant, laundromat, hair salon, and gift shop featuring art and photography by local artists.

Getting to Central Coast Adventures requires a flight or ferry to Bella Coola, then a ferry between the city and Denny Island.
www.centralcoastadventures.ca

Duval Point Lodge

Duval Island, on the northern end of Johnstone Strait, is directly in the path of British Columbia's salmon migration. The Lodge's protected bay covers four acres of land, including one acre of waterfront leased from the Gwa'sala Nakwaxda'xw First Nations. In 2010, after relocating their family, including all five children, to Port Hardy, David and Lisa Beckman purchased the remote 21-year-old Lodge. Duval Island, on the northern end of Johnstone Strait, is directly in the path of British Columbia's salmon migration.

Duval Point Lodge has accommodations both on land and floating. Their fishing is self-guided with local guides available. Cabins run on propane with diesel-powered electricity, and a battery back-up. Anglers bring and cook their own food. This simplicity is overwhelmed by its natural beauty and good fishing.

Floating lodges have up to four bedrooms equipped with two or three single beds, two bathrooms, a fully equipped kitchen, and living room warmed by a wood burning fireplace. Bed linen, blankets, towels, dishes, cutlery, and a barbecue is supplied. Fishing in Goletas Chanel offers Chinook, the other species of salmon, and halibut. A large rock attracts orcas that come for a belly scratch. Eagle fish with the anglers or perch near the fish-cleaning table, located on a floating dock, for tasty scraps. Harbor seals and black bear are local residents. Most Duval Point Lodge anglers are experienced fisherman, but every level is welcomed. Anglers are required to have a safe boater's license. The Lodge has twelve 16½-foot welded aluminum boats with 30 HP Yamaha 4-stroke motors. Each 2-person boat has swivel seats, manual downriggers, a depth sounder, rods with gear and tackle, and a net. A small fee is charged for extras, but the basics are included with the boat.

At the end of the fishing day, anglers can relax on the deck, barbecue their catch, or gather around the lodge's fireplace to cook dinner in a well-equipped modern kitchen. Anglers can choose to fish the evening bite, visit with new friends in the lodge, or call it a day.

General Manager Jessica and her partner Eric see that dock staff clean each boat, fill the engine with gas, restock tackle boxes, and supply anglers with bait for the next day. Anglers are encouraged to bring children who are happily offered special rates.

Location is everything. While good fishing is minutes from the dock, Duval Point Lodge's boats motor within a 10-mile radius. The "witch's" tree, light green moss known as witch's hair, is very productive for all species of salmon. A 20-minute water taxi operated by Gwa'sala Nakwaxda'xw Nation provides transfers from Bear Cove near Port Hardy.

(Source: Duval Point Lodge)

www.duvalpointlodge.com

Haa-Nee-Naa Lodge

Located between two of North America's most productive salmon rivers, the Skeena and the Nass, Dundas Island sits directly on the migratory path of millions of Pacific salmon. Haa-Nee-Naa Lodge guests get first crack at the fish making their way to local rivers along the British Columbia coastline to their natal spawning grounds.

As the only floating sport fishing resort located on a cove on remote Dundas Island, 35 miles northwest of Prince Rupert, Haa-Nee-Naa Lodge is one of British Columbia's northern-most saltwater salmon fishing lodges. Offering fishing for Chinook salmon, halibut, and lingcod fishing, they also offer saltwater coho fly fishing.

Each guest room is furnished with a twin and a double bed, and features ensuite bathrooms, direct patio access, and wonderful views of the Alaskan Panhandle. A spacious living area, which shares the stunning view, offers leather sofas. A library is available for movies or books or there is the option of relaxing on one of the large patio docks.

Haa-Nee-Naa Lodge provides gourmet meals, which includes New Zealand rack of lamb, fresh seafood pastas, Alberta Grade A Prime

Rib or filet mignon. Tasty appetizers, freshly baked rolls, and decadent desserts accompany all dinners.

Fishing is done primarily by mooching (slow trolling) cut-plug herring behind 10'6 graphite rods with Canadian-style single action reels. The lodge finds fishing slow back eddies along kelp beds and rock walls at depths of 10-35 pulls (20-70 feet) is an extremely effective method for targeting aggressive Chinook and coho salmon. For those who prefer to fish with a geared level wind reel, the Lodge provides these outfits. Also available to anglers is a selection of Sage 8-weight fly fishing rods and reels.

Bottom fishing enthusiasts can target the vast array of bottom dwellers with the Lodge's Stout 6-foot halibut rods, and Penn level wind reels loaded with 50-pound no-stretch Tuff Line.

Haa-Nee-Naa Lodge clean and filleted the angler's catch throughout the day. Fillets are vacuum packed and flash frozen. At the end of the trip, the angler's catch will be packed and labeled in a waxed-box.

Dundas Island, rich in scenery and wildlife, lies between the waters of Dixon Entrance East and Chatham Sound scenery on the Pacific Coast. Its calm protected coves, inlets and bays stretch massive kelp beds extend to ocean pounded rocks and beautiful white sand beaches.

It is not uncommon to watch pods of orcas swim within yards of your boat or majestic bald eagles soar in the skies above. Dundas Island is also on the direct migratory path of feeding humpback whales. It is a common experience to see these magnificent creatures breaching and bubble feeding as they make their journey south. Other local residents include porpoises, seals, sea lions, otters, swimming coastal wolves, and many bird species.

The plane ride from Vancouver International Airport to Prince Rupert is two hours. From Digby Island it a 35-mile float plane ride to Haa-Nee-Naa Lodge.

(Source Haa Nee Naa Lodge)

www.haaneenaa.com

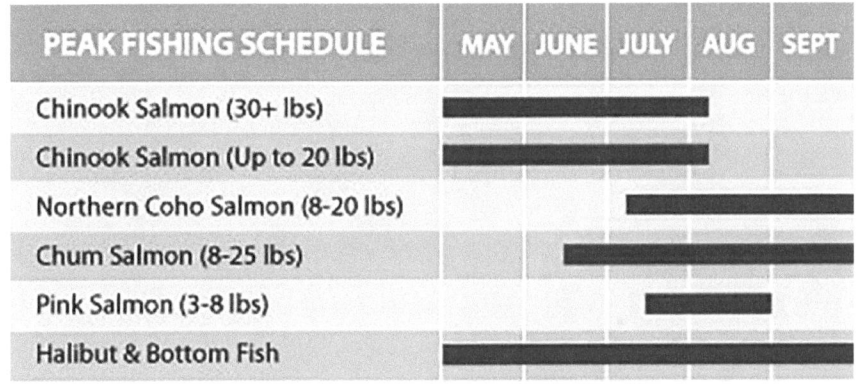

Hakai Pass Lodge

Located north of Rivers Inlet and south of Prince Rupert, Hakai Pass is the central coast location of Hakai Lodge. In 1972, founder Dwaine Howard scouted British Columbia between Prince Rupert and Campbell River. Scenic, well-protected, conveniently located, and with a long, productive fishing season, Hakai Pass was his choice location. It was also protected from commercial fishing, which insured a larger abundance of fish.

Set in unspoiled beauty with white sand beaches, sparkling waters, lush forest, and hundreds of unexplored islands and islets, Howard established Hakai Lodge. In 1984, Byron Swanson joined the Lodge expanding its staff and equipment. The eight cabin, hosting up to a dozen anglers, atmosphere was family-oriented, comfortable, and included Wi-Fi.

When Howard retired, Clyde Carlson stepped in to take his place. As a company owner of the regional seaplanes flying anglers, he was well acquainted with the area. Since 2010, both the lodge and fleet of Boston Whalers have been updated. 40 years later, second and third generations of families are returning to Hakai Lodge.

A unique combination of weather, geography, and other conditions create perfect conditions for the angler to enjoy Chinook salmon fishing conditions not found elsewhere.

Many of the trophy-sized Chinook caught over the years at Hakai Lodge are headed for nearby Rivers Inlet. Rivers Inlet is world renowned for its record sized fish, the largest on record being a whopping 124 pounds. Those fish migrate through the Pass on their final journey to the Kilbella and Chuckwalla Rivers located at the head of Rivers Inlet.

A trip to Hakai Lodge includes round-trip air from Vancouver, all meals, use of 17-foot Montauk Boston Whalers with 30 or 40 HP 4-stroke Yamaha motors, all fishing tackle with bait, daily housekeeping, and cleaning, packing, and freezing your catch.

(Source: Hakai Pass Lodge)

www.hakai-lodge.com

Ole's Lodge at Hakai Pass

Anchored in the sheltered waters of Barney Bay, Hakai Pass, Ole's Floating Fishing Lodge offers comfort, privacy, and convenience expected on a British Columbia fishing trip.

The day begins with whiffing the aroma of freshly baked goodies inviting anglers to a robust continental breakfast, one substantial enough to hold them through the morning bite. It's all about the salmon fishing at Ole's Hakai Pass Fishing Lodge. They stagger meal times to take full advantage of tidal changes, which means anglers are always on the water at the peak the bite.

During fishing time, the chef sets Dungeness crab pots for a fresh seafood appetizer. Following a snack of salmon and halibut ceviche or Indian candy, meals are served with fine dinner wines and anglers can enjoy everything from juicy steaks to sushi to barbecue. There are cream puffs or maybe a chocolate fondue for dessert. The spacious dining area is a gathering place for guests to reminiscence, tell fish stories, and enjoy the company of other dedicated anglers.

Ole's provides each angler with a private, clean and comfortable ensuite guest room hosting 1-3 people. Housekeeping is provided.

Hakai Pass' pristine waters offer superb salmon fishing. Trophy-sized salmon funnel through Hakai Pass from the open Pacific Ocean en route to Rivers Inlet.

British Columbia's central west coast is still inaccessible. Ole's Hakai Pass Fishing Lodge offers solitude and a true Canadian wilderness holiday that includes spectacular scenery and wildlife including marine mammals and birds.

To hone fishing skills, Ole's comprehensive fishing clinic offers expertise on cut plug or whole herring bait, tying knots, trolling speed, and patterns to proper netting skills, all productive fishing techniques. From dawn to dusk anglers have unlimited access to salmon and halibut fishing from new, custom made, self-bailing, unsinkable 18-foot welded aluminum boats. Powered by new, clean, quiet 40 HP 4-stroke outboards, these fishing boats are equipped with Lowrance fish finders, radios, and top-of-the-line fishing gear.

Barney Point and the Racetrack salmon fishing grounds are located within five minutes of the dock. Ole's salmon fishing charters uses Daiwa "knuckle-busters" or Penn 220 level wind reel. They also provide comfortable, weatherproof floater suits, and rubber boots. Unique to Ole's, they even include a fishing license.

A spacious dry room is available for outerwear so anglers have a dry start to each fishing day. Before you're even up in the morning the staff will have warmed up the boat motors for you and set up your tackle and bait requirements for the tide.

At the end of the day Ole's staff will clean, fillet, vacuum pack your catch. It is then flash-frozen and wax-boxed for the trip home. They restock, refuel, and clean the boat so you can relax and enjoy the comforts of the floating fishing lodge and the camaraderie of fellow fishing guests.

Getting to Ole's is by Seair Seaplanes from Vancouver. The trip is less than two hours.
(Source: Ole's Hakai Pass)
www.ole.ca

Nimmo Bay Wilderness Resort

Considered as the British Columbia's resort that invented heli-fishing along the province's coast, the 30-year-old family owned and operated luxurious resort revolves around activities based on the use of helicopters. Located in foothills of Mount Stephens in the Great Bear Rainforest, the resort is an exclusive fly fishing and wilderness adventure destination. Founded more than 30 years ago, the resort is a mecca for anglers, mariners and adventurers alike. With the use of helicopters and boats, Nimmo Bay customizes adventure holidays to match anyone's wildest desires.

The resort was built in harmony with nature, with half of the resort floating in the peaceful bay and the other half center on a small outcropping of land. A stunning waterfall flows through the resort's centre. Access to the Nimmo Bay is limited to boat, float plane and helicopter. Daily wilderness and helicopter adventures give guests access to 50,000 square miles of untouched wilderness.

This adventure is for the experienced fly-fisher as well as those who would like to learn. Anglers can bring their own rods and reels or use Nimmo Bay gear.

Experienced guides take anglers to isolated streams filled with wild salmon, steelhead, Dolly Varden, char and rainbow, and cutthroat trout. The helicopter remains with the angler all day providing access to 50,000 square miles of terrain, including more than 50 rivers and streams. Nimmo Bay practices catch and release and the use of single barbless hooks.

(Source: Nimmo Bay Wilderness Resort)

www.nimmobay.com

Prince Rupert Foggy Point Charters

Anglers visiting the northern coastal city of Prince Rupert can hire a variety of boats and guides for day or overnight fishing adventures from Foggy Point Charters

www.foggypoint.com

Shearwater Resort and Marina

Located in British Columbia's Great Bear Rainforest, Shearwater Resort has a variety of options for both the angler and the eco-adventurer. Recent additions include The Water's Edge Hideaway, a floating home overlooking Shearwater Resort and bay and One Ten Shearwater, a private 2-bedroom home overlooking the resort and harbor.

Other accommodations include the popular The Captain's Cottage, a private 2-bedroom cottage, Shearwater Lodge, cozy and comfortable, and the Cedar Lodge, a traditional lodge approach to coastal accommodations. There is also a Shearwater RV Park & Campground.

Shearwater Resort offers 26 anglers extra-large beds with a private bathroom, television, and coffee maker. Full housekeeping service is provided and turn-down service is available. The lodge has a custom-designed lounge that includes a pool table, poker table, and wet bar surrounding a river rock fireplace.

Their Coast Guard Certified 17-foot fiberglass Hourston boats, with full windshields and convertible canvas tops, are powered by 60 HP Yamaha outboards. Fishing gear includes 10 ½-foot Daiwa rods with Shimano 2000 GT reels and Scotty downriggers. All boats are equipped with digital fish finders and VHF radios. Floater coats, raingear, and rubber boots are provided. Shearwater fishing packages are designed to meet the needs of all anglers wishing to tailor their trip around their own ability and comfort. To achieve this they offer fully guided, semi-guided fishing trips, and self-guided fishing trips.

Fishing "hot spots" are located 5-45 minutes from the resort in surrounding protected channels and inlets. Regardless of the angler's choice, Shearwater also has a fish master within communicable range and a local fishing guide keeping an eye on Shearwater fishing lodge guests.

Unique to Shearwater is the opportunity to take an incredible adventure in search of the rare kermode or "spirit bear." This recessive gene black bear is rarely sighted and known only to exist in the Great Bear Rainforest.

Getting to Shearwater is either by plane from Vancouver's South Terminal to Bella Coola, then taking a short water taxi to Denny Island, or arrival by private boat, plane, or BC Ferry in Bella Coola.
(Source Shearwater Resort)
www.shearwater.ca

Sund's Lodge on Malcolm Island

Malcolm Island is the intimate 40-acre setting for Sund's Lodge. Small and family-oriented, it holds a maximum of 24 anglers in 12 charming cabins overlooking Blackfish Sound, a short BC Ferry ride from Point McNeil on Vancouver Island.

Anglers can fish to their heart's content, explore in a sea kayak, bike into town, or nap in a hammock. The experience is warm and attentive with service that will make you feel both at home.

Amenities include: two hot tubs, a sauna, bicycles, sea kayaks, a golf practice range, hiking paths, satellite television, a pool table, and wireless Internet throughout the entire property.

All species of salmon are found within minutes of the dock. Blackfish Sound offers calm, protected waters. From the area's natural beauty with rolling mountains at Vancouver Island northern tip, to 5-course dining, to the 40-acre resort, to the incredible fishing at 40-acre Sund's Lodge provides an adventure for the whole family.

Their fleet consists of eight 23-foot Aluminum Chambered Boats, regarded as one of the safest, most comfortable fishing boats on the market.

A Mary L. Peachin Adventure

Cow bells and staff cheering outside your door is the 4:15 morning wake up call. It's dark outside. After an evening of fine wine and dining, only the urgency of catching a tyee can rustle me out of bed. I've fished British Columbia's coastline for well over a decade and have only come close, a pound or two shy of the fabled 30-pound entry qualification to this exclusive club.

Storm fronts move quickly between Port McNeil, Vancouver Island, and the fishing grounds of Baronete Pass. Sheets of rain are silhouetted between the lush horizons of the Coast Mountains. We are fishing waters located adjacent to Johnstone Strait and Blackfish Bay near Georgia Straight.

While fishing for Chinook near Parson's Island "The Wall" drop off, less than five minutes after lowering a sardine-baited hook on a downrigger, the line tugged gently. Chinook are unpredictable. Most will make an initial fierce run, a few will jump, and some swim toward you until seeing the boat motivates them to take off. This one waited until he neared the boat. Most of the salmon run were "teeners", or Chinook weighing in the high teens.

Sund's aluminum boats, powered by a Yamaha 250 plus a trolling engine, are custom-made and average 23 feet. They have a cabin and the luxury of a head. Most of their fishing is done with a Shimano mooching reel on a Laminglas rod.

When fishing the bite is off, and on a day at "The Slide" when I limited out (two Chinook a day or a total of four) by 6:30 AM, there were some awesome sights. Minke, orca, and humpback whales ply these waters. Pacific white-sided and Dall's porpoise sometimes swim in the boat's bow wake. Murres dive, bald eagles soar, and shore birds wade in quiet bays.

Successful anglers will frequently fight salmon during the early morning bite, then afternoon jig for "chickens." These smaller halibut, those in the 25-45 pound range, make for better eating.

On a day of fishing with guide Geoffrey Duddridge, and Diana and Brian Gage from Camas, Washington, we had some interesting and exciting afternoon action.

After hookup, the salmon jumped in the air before running endlessly. Coho are more likely to jump, and while they hadn't migrated seasonally through the area, there were a few around. Geoff knew from the pull that a harbor seal had grabbed my salmon, and he was heading into a bed of bull kelp. Chasing it with the boat, Geoffrey prepared to throw Pepsi cans to scare the seal so he would release his clutch on my salmon. The seal won.

Craycroft Point was good to us. In seven years of guiding, Geoffrey had never had a triple hookup. Brian and I were fishing the outside downriggers and Diana was on the flat line. Soon after they hooked up, my rod also bent. It was bedlam. We each followed our fish exchanging places and moving rods around and over one another to prevent a tangle.

While I was mooching for salmon, my husband David was an hour-and-a-half north wading for elusive sea run cutthroat. The only access to the Ahta River is by boat. This keeps its rushing waters pristine and the fish unwary.

Local anglers sometimes call coastal sea-run cutthroat trout tinsels, harvest, or yellowbellies. Sporty on a lightweight fly rod, they enter various spawning rivers to feed on springtime salmon fry or fall salmon eggs. While nomadic, sea run trout spawn and return to the same system.

Armed with bear spray, guide Shaun Vanderberg and David bushwhacked an overgrown but marked trail along Bond Sound's Ahta River on the British Columbia mainland. Bear scat along the trail was so fresh "we could smell it". Shaun and David released a dozen 16- to 18-inch fish along with two sizable rainbows. Shaun tied his own flies and used a Mickey Finn clouser, an attractor minnow patterned fly and a custom-made "bubbler" minnow, similar to a mudler.

While David was cheerfully casting dry flies at jumping cutthroat, I was still on the decade-long search for that magical 30-pound tyee. Sund's Lodge didn't disappoint. It was the third and final full day of fishing when I hooked into a big one. He didn't look like a tyee, but before bleeding it (for better taste), we weighed it. It was 30 pounds and not an ounce more. There were four witnesses just in case the fish, after being bled, lost some weight and went under 30 pounds. It didn't.

Avid anglers will appreciate the amenities provided by this family-owned and -operated lodge. Spanning 40 acres on Malcolm Island, 12 cabins host a maximum of 24 guests. Anglers can fish the entire 3 or 5-day package, explore the coastline in a sea kayak, or bicycle 10 miles into the small Finnish town of Sointula. Founded in 1901 as a socialist commune, Sointula's 800 residents are proud of their heritage. The name means "place of harmony."

Sund's cedar cabins are built with wood locally harvested. Comfortable beds, covered with down comforters and 600 thread-count Egyptian cotton sheets, feel great at the end of a 12-hour fishing day. All cabins have a gorgeous view of Blackfish Sound. The Sund family has a herd of groomed alpaca that mow their acre-size lawn overlooking the Sound.

If you have the time, there are two hot tubs, a sauna, bicycles, sea kayaks, a golf practice range, horse shoes, hiking paths, satellite TV, pool table, and wireless internet through the property.

Lunch is different than that found in most fishing camps.

Instead of packing your own lunch or waiting for a boat to come out at lunch hour, Sund's has a "burger boat" that has a gas grill cooking hot dogs and hamburgers.

Another day, the staff greets you on a nearby beach with a glass of wine and a first course of freshly caught Dungeness crab. But first, there is a lesson on preparing the live crab. The Chef has a table-clothed table with pull pork sandwiches, salad, and his scrumptious homemade lemon squares for desserts.

Fine wine and spirits are included in your stay. They can be enjoyed while dining on Chef Paul Shand's, formerly of renowned Sooke Harbour House, gourmet 5-course cuisine. He is not your typical fishing lodge chef. Servers and bartenders Sheena, Amber, and Jamie are so friendly, hugs are forthcoming when you say goodbye.

None of this would be possible without the leadership and friendliness of Scott Sund. He bought the lodge from his father, Dave, about eight years ago. Along with his wife Heather and three young children, their goal is to make you feel as though you were part of the family. And they do a mighty fine job!

A Mary L. Peachin Adventure

Oh, give me grace to catch a fish so big that even I, when talking afterwards, may have no need to lie. -Anonymous

Mucho Don, a studly alpaca, spends most of his life servicing a dozen females. Life is blissful for the harem that spends much of their day sleeping or munching on a grassy hillside at Sund's Lodge. The alpacas, several with newborns, plus one odd llama, roam 40 acres of land between lodge cabins and dockside, where guided fishing boats wait for enthusiastic anglers.

But Mucho's active sex life pales in comparison to the overall experience of guests who visit Sund's Lodge to fish for salmon, kayak coves in the Strait, or admire playful killer whales or black bears who grub for algae on beaches during low tide.

Twenty years ago, Dave Sund, fed up with his office job, sold two rental properties to chase his dream – a love of fishing. A realtor showed him an available lodge on Malcolm Island, five miles east of the northern tip of Vancouver Island. Sund saw it, fell in love with the place, and the next day was a proud new landowner and lodge operator.

Not far from the village of Sointula, a Finnish village that dates back to 1903 with a name meaning harmony, Sund's Lodge sits on 40 acres. The First Nations Kwakiutl band living on surrounding islands considered Malcolm an evil place because of the way it pinnacled out of Queen Charlotte Strait. Superstition didn't prevent their foraging into the wooded landscape to gather cedar trees to use for their highly prized carvings.

In the early 1960s, Malcolm Island was mostly embraced by Vietnam draft dodgers who spent their time hand building the original lodge. They hung around for several decades.

Today the wood cabin lodge with tastefully designed rooms

operates in secluded Blackfish Sound near the route of Alaska cruise ship plying the Inside Passage.

Dave and Sally Sund, with their son Scott and his wife Heather, are celebrating more than 25 years of operating this small lodge. There is nothing rustic about the place. Appointments exude a personal touch and to name just a few, include Dave's personal collection of duck decoys, couches upholstered with "Gone fishin'" motif, a candy bar gift basket in each cabin next to a personalized welcome card with a book about the history of the lodge and its philosophy of customer service.

When guests aren't fishing, kayaking, or wildlife viewing, the friendly staff is looking out for their every need. In fact, after a day on the water the staff even brings drinks and appetizers to the hot tub or golf hitting area.

Sund's Lodge is prepared for the healthy appetite, and the food is not only plentiful, it is gourmet. The staff includes two young chefs who know their cooking and for better or for worse (to those who might be weight conscious), make homemade bread and scrumptious desserts for lunch and dinner.

Five 26-foot Aluminum Chambered Boats, each with a 225 horsepower Mercury engine plus a trolling motor, wait for loading dockside at the crack of dawn.

Our first day of fishing was a challenging and less-than-successful 12 hours. Guide Geoff Millar uses anchovies and hoochie lures in a valiant effort to get fish to bite in unusual windy conditions. Some of us are more distracted by a pod of killer whales and fishing bald eagles that are more plentiful than sea gulls. Lodge guests during my visit were almost exclusively fathers with their sons. One day I fished with Terry and son Marc who reeled in almost identical 24-pound Chinook salmon. They shared the honor of dining in the "big fish" chair, reserved for the fisher that catches the biggest fish of the day.

When it was time for lunch, we joined the staff, Mark, Vivian and Pat Wilson, who wore white chef's outfits, meeting in a secluded cove for a Dungeness crab cookout. But first, Dave gave us a crab-cooking lesson. Like lobster, crab is prepared alive. Avoiding their sharp pinchers requires a deft hand. Cleaning them is a new education for most of us and the crabs, just raised from the lodge's crab pot, are so tender that we cracked them campfire-side with our hands.

Another day, I fish with John and his son Ryan Meehan. When Ryan wasn't catching fish, he was in the hold sleeping. What a day he had, he missed the "big chair" by a few ounces to Stewart, whose 11-year-old grandson Jordan, the youngest boy in camp, decided he preferred spending his time helping dock crew rather than fishing.

The father and son group had a great time. Aside from the fishing, those who wanted to lay back could take in some of the other activities. There are two hot tubs, a pool table, golf practice tee, or they could lounge around the fire beachside fire pit watching the sun go down. For the more energetic, there are bicycles and sea kayaks. Great facilities, salmon fishing, and incredible service make this wilderness experience unique and wonderful.

The fishing season at Sund's Lodge starts in May with trips into the beautiful inlets of mainland British Columbia. The summer months of June through September are spent fishing the bountiful waters of Blackfish Sound for all five species of salmon and chasing after the huge Chinooks swimming south through the Inside Passage.

In the month of September, the lodge provides one of the most beautiful multi-sport adventures in British Columbia. During September, guests watch grizzly bears, view Orca whales, hike a 10-kilometer trail on Malcolm Island's northern shore, explore abandoned Indian villages, or just relax around the property at the Lodge.

A Mary L. Peachin Adventure

British Columbia is noted for five species of salmon migrating along coastal waters throughout the summer. Bottom fishers favor BC's numerous flats where they can jig for halibut. But where can you go to fish, a lodge that offers both saltwater and freshwater fly fishing? Not too many places. If you include luxury accommodations, gourmet cuisine, and cheerful, excellent service, it's doubtful there are any that can compete with Sund's Lodge.

Cow bells and staff cheering outside your door is the 4:15am morning wake up call. It's dark outside. After an evening of fine wine and dining, only the urgency to catch a tyee can rustle me out of bed. I've fished British Columbia's coastline for more than a decade and have only come close, a pound or two shy of the fabled 30-pound entry qualification to an exclusive club.

Storm fronts move quickly between Port McNeil, Vancouver Island and the fishing grounds of Baronete Pass. Sheets of rain are silhouetted between the lush horizons of the Coast Mountains. We are fishing waters located adjacent to Johnstone Strait and Blackfish Bay near the Georgia Straights.

While fishing for Chinook, also known as spring or king, near Parson's Island "The Wall" drop off, it was less than five minutes after lowering a sardine-baited hook on a downrigger with, when the line tugged gently. Chinook are unpredictable. Most will make an initial fierce run, a few will jump, and some swim toward you until seeing the boat motivates them to take off at high speed. Most of the run were "teeners" or Chinook weighing in the high teens.

Sund's aluminum boats, powered by a Yamaha 250 plus a trolling engine, are custom made and average 23 feet. They have a cabin and the luxury of a head. Most of the fishing is done with a Shimano mooching reel on a Laminglas rod.

When fishing the bite is off, and the day at "The Slide" after I limited out (two Chinook a day or a total of four) by 6:30 AM, there were some awesome sights. Minke, orca, and humpback whales play these waters. Pacific white-sided and Dall's porpoise sometimes swim in the boat's bow wake. Murres dive, bald eagles soar, and shore birds wade in quiet bays.

Successful anglers will frequently fight salmon during the early morning bite then in the afternoon jig for "chickens." The smaller halibut, those in the 25-45 pound range, make for better eating.

On a day of fishing with guide Geoffrey Duddridge, and Diana and Brian Gage from Camas, Washington, we had some interesting and exciting afternoon action.

After hooking up, the salmon jumped in the air before running endlessly. Coho are more typical jumpers and while they hadn't seasonally migrated through the area, there were a few around. Geoff knew from the pull that a harbor seal had grabbed my salmon and he was heading into a bed of bull kelp. Chasing it with the boat, Geoffrey prepared to throw Pepsi cans to scare the seal so he would release his clutch on my salmon. The seal won.

Craycroft Point was good to us. In seven years of guiding,

Geoffrey had never had a triple hookup. Brian and I were fishing the outside downriggers, Diana was on the flat line. As they hooked up, my rod also bent. It was bedlam. We each followed our fish exchanging places and moving rods around and over one another to prevent a tangle.

While I was mooching for salmon, my husband David was an hour and a half north wading for elusive sea run cutthroat. The only access to the Ahta River is by boat keeping rushing waters pristine and the fish unwary.

Local anglers sometimes call coastal sea-run cutthroat trout tinsels, harvest, or yellowbellies. Sporty on a lightweight fly rod, they enter various spawning rivers to feed on springtime salmon fry or fall salmon eggs. While nomadic, sea run trout spawn and return to the same system. Armed with bear spray, guide Shaun Vanderberg and David bushwhacked an overgrown but marked trail along Bond Sound's Ahta River on the British Columbia mainland. Bear scat along the trail was so fresh "we could smell it". Shaun and David released a dozen 16- to 18-inch fish along with two sizable rainbows.

Shaun tied his own flies and used a Mickey Finn clouser, an attractor minnow patterned fly and a custom-made "bubbler" minnow, similar to a mudler.

While David was cheerfully casting dry flies at jumping cutthroat, I was still on the decade-long search for that magical 30-pound tyee. Sund's Lodge didn't disappoint. It was the third and final full day of fishing when I hooked into a big one. He didn't look like a tyee, but before bleeding it (for better taste), we weighed it. 30 pounds and not an ounce more. There were four witnesses just in case the fish, after being bled, lost some weight and went under 30 pounds. It didn't.

West Sport Fishing Lodge

Formerly known as King Pacific Lodge, in 2014, George and Lisa Culbertson purchased, opened, and renamed the 3-story lodge as West Sport Fishing. Prior to the Culbertson opening, the Lodge operated as one of British Columbia's most luxurious. Its wide array of activities included heli-fly fishing and late summer kermode (spirit bear) viewing. West Sport now operates as an upscale fishing lodge with multiple options for both guiding and self-guiding for multiple species of fish.

Doug Olander, *Sport Fishing* magazine editor-in-chief, found that

"Looking for fish was not exactly like searching for a needle in a haystack. The salmon bite, periodically wide open, also gave us the chance for bonus catches of lingcod, greenling, and rockfish while we were drift-jigging."

The contemporary 34 guest floating fishing and adventure lodge includes round-trip airfare from Vancouver, unlimited fishing, and delicious meals. The welcoming staff includes those from nearby local communities.

There are three options for fishing. Self-Guided anglers will be assisted by West Sport's "Fish Master" offering water assistance, dock instruction, and evening seminars on information necessary to catch fish. All Instructed anglers receive five hours of on-water fishing instruction each full day of their trip.

Fully guided anglers receive 10 to 12 hours of fishing with the guide's undivided attention to detail.

West Sport Fishing's "King Pacific Lodge" at Milbanke Sound is a British Columbia family owned salmon lodge company created as a testament to the friendship of the many anglers and friends George and Lisa Cuthbert have come to know over the past 25 years.

In addition to deluxe double occupancy accommodations with private bathrooms, gourmet dinners are served with complementary beer and wine. There is also unlimited use of fishing boats and equipment including all tackle, bait, waterproof outerwear and fishing boots. Professional care features fish fillet, cutting, vacuum packaging, then freezing and crating catch for your return flight.

A Mary L. Peachin Adventure

A departing guest, her baggage dockside, murmured, "I'm jealous, you're arriving and we're leaving." As we warmed ourselves by the cozy fireplace, our attention drifted to the great mountain views surrounding Barnard Harbour. Adventurous activities we could experience during the following three days at what was then King Pacific Lodge had one semblance of civilization: an occasional cruise ship plying through Campania Sound bound for Alaska.

Six sleepy anglers had wandered to the lobby of Vancouver's airport Fairmont hotel at the crack of dawn. We handed our 30-pound baggage allocation to a representative from the lodge then proceeded to our Air Canada flight. Several hours later we landed in Prince Rupert, a city close to the northern border of British Columbia. There, we were greeted by a driver who shuttled us a short distance to a nearby dock where we boarded a Harbour Air floatplane.

An hour later, the pilot glided into the harbor, idling his props, as he taxied to the dock of the elegant resort, a converted (with no expense spared) former U.S. naval barge. The lodge is located between the cities of Bella Bella and Prince Rupert, the land of Tsimshian First Nation's band. It is anchored to the bank of Princess Royal Island, an island designated part of the Great Bear Rainforest. The lodge was towed to Milbanke Sound after being purchased by George and Lisa Cuthbert.

Hideo 'Joe' Morita, a son of the founder of Sony, bought an existing lodge, converted it to staff housing, and then built the adjacent luxury resort. Constructed of natural materials including wood beams and slate floors, the main room of the lodge features a massive 2-story stone fireplace, a sectioned dining room, video and game room, a treadmill, and a spa with a hot tub and offers massage therapy.

The front porch leads to the dock facing the westerly view of the mountains surrounding the harbor. Upstairs, 18 suite-size bedrooms have king-size duvet-covered beds. Wall-to-wall windows have views of the harbor or rainforest. Bathrooms offer a full shower plus large soaker tubs. A basket of amenities includes a nubby roller for sore fishing muscles.

An active adventure destination, King Pacific Lodge offers interpretive hikes among 1,000-year-old hemlocks, ocean kayaking through fiords and inlets, and the opportunity to search for the indigenous Kermode "White Spirit" black bear. The bear carries a recessive gene, an anomaly sacred to the First Nations band. It is considered good luck to have a rare viewing experience

Each meal is a gourmet adventure. Between courses, each guest is given the opportunity to decide between going fishing on 17-foot guided Campion boats, kayaking, hiking, beachcombing, or searching for grizzlies and viewing glaciers from the lodge's helicopter. Between smoked scallops and our entree of fresh salmon, we are asked if we'd like to see a river otter with four pups who sometimes hang out behind the floating lodge. The table is deserted as we all got a close up view of the otters.

Our first stop is the dry room where each of us would gear up in a bright red Mustang survival suit (for warmth and safety) and a pair of rubber boots. I've come to try my rod at salmon fishing but en route to Eclipse Point, we make a detour to observe a rock occupied by stellar sea lions. The bulls roar as the boat approaches. Females, lying on a separate rock, seem content to be defended by the males. The stench of their droppings – whew, we held our breath.

Guide Wyler Dundax is a member of the village of Hartley Bay (Gutga'ata) First Nations band. His small village is located at the entrance to Douglas Channel. He drops squid-looking "hoochies" on a downrigger to about 40 feet as we troll along the inlets and fiords near rainforest banks.

Suddenly a waterspout appears. Humpback whales inhabit these waters, gently swimming until sounding with a "tail up". It is a slow afternoon of fishing. We release two Chinook and one coho. Soaring eagles and whale encounters have made the time fly.

Early the next morning, Guide Ronnie Ludvigson and I follow two humpbacks cruising the bank. "Smells like they ate rotten cabbage" as we get a whiff downwind from their spouting. Whale halitosis travels a long way.

It's been several weeks since larger Chinook have migrated through the area. We hook into several 15-pounders. This is a good sign that another school is coming. We also release several jumping coho and a pink "humpie."

Ronnie is watching "bait balls" on his fish finder as a Department of Ocean and Fisheries boat approaches. They are patrolling to check for fishing licenses, barbless hooks, and anglers exceeding their catching limits of two fish per species. Identifying us as a King Pacific Lodge boat, they continue on. They know we follow the rules.

Betraying their majestic size, eagles chirped like songbirds. When we returned at noon, a rookie angler, Sarah English, has caught a 30-pound Chinook called a tyee. Taking a break from fishing, we again set out for some whale watching, searching for the kermode and black bear scavenging on beaches, and check out a 50-year old tug boat wreck.

The north coast area near Prince Rupert experiences large, powerful tides, some which can rise 24-feet. There is a 4-foot change in water level every hour with two high and two low tides each day.

Our final day brings one of life's biggest fishing thrills. Angler Carl Duncan and I climb into the lodge's Bell 206 helicopter with pilot Paul Tosczak and head fishing guide Wayne Boles. Lifting off the dock we fly at an altitude of 1,000 feet as we fly Whale Channel past Gill Island to the Quall River. The helicopter lands in a grassy meadow blooming with spring flowers. Pink salmon have just begun their spawn up the river. Using 8-weight fly rods with pink "show-girls" flies (pink fluff that, in water, resembles a leech.), we wade to our waist in the sandy bottom of the river. A pink hits the first fly and circles around me in the clear water. He is a male with a big hump, sea lice are still attached to his scales indicating he is a recent migrate from the ocean, fresh and strong still for the battle up the river where he will spawn and die.

Several strands of grass float by me. Wayne nonchalantly says "guess we have a bear upstream." When the spawn is in full swing, bears head to this river to fish. We see only a few bear today. Wayne had his only Kermode bear sighting along the Quall.

An owl hooting above the rush of the stream was suddenly interrupted by the sound of a large crash. Was that thunder, I wondered on this glorious sunny day? "No, just another avalanche," I'm told. The higher peaks of the Coast range are still snowcapped.

As we continue to fish, moving the helicopter to another location after significantly disturbing a school of salmon, Wayne tells me these fish have never encountered an angler is this remote site. They aren't really interested in feeding, they are just pissed off and snapping at whatever fly we put in front of them. In a few days, schools of coho will run the river.

This time a bear interrupts our fishing and we board the helicopter for a flight down Whale Channel past Hartley Bay. The time had passed too quickly before it was time to depart. Another option would have been to fish for cutthroat and rainbow native trout on the Lowe or Klewnuggett lakes, a 15-30 minute flight, but the time was late.

Our final day we woke early to kayak around the banks of Barnard Harbour into Cameron cove. Small Dungeness crabs scurry sideways along the rocky bottom, newborn salmon along with schools of smolts, and Eagles sit perched on the tops of fir trees. The distinctive cry of the loon echoes across the water. All too soon our floatplane arrives. Our adventure is over. (Author's note: King Pacific Lodge was purchased and moved to Milbanke Sound where it now operates as West Coast Fishing.)

A Mary L. Peachin Adventure

Fly Fishing for Pink Salmon in the Great Bear Rainforest

Hey, grizzly! Grabbing his bear spray, fly fishing guide Logan Wilkins shouted, "Patricia, start walking slowly down the beach...NOW!" Resting against a fallen tree trunk at the beach's edge, river riffles muffled Logan's words. An immense tree blocked Pat's view of the grizzly standing on the log, peering at us from its rainforest sanctuary. Oblivious to any danger, Pat instinctively responded by crouching as we walked slowly up the beach toward the river. The bear reacted to Logan's command by retreating into the forest.

Wading Khutz River for pink salmon, known as humpies because of their rounded back, I got the message when I saw Logan with bear spray in hand. Although my thighs continued to quiver after the incident, I remained fishing in the River. The encounter had lasted only minutes.

After all, we were casting into the bears' fishing hole, one they use each fall to bulk up before winter hibernation by feasting on migrating salmon. Just minutes before, two grizzlies had ambled along the beach toward us. At Logan's alert, we watched as the bears, after spotting us, detoured from their salmon fishing grounds into the brush.

While sharing the fishing grounds of grizzlies may have added some excitement, fly fishing the Khutz was more than just another great fishing experience. We enjoyed one of those Great Bear

Rainforest rare days when the sun was shining, the River's cold water was crystal clear, and the temperature an unusual high of 70 degrees. As I shed my long underwear, I wondered if the grizzlies might be hunkering down in the alders to avoid the heat of the day before they emerged when the temperature began to drop. Throughout the day, we had, somewhat nervously, scanned the beach and hillsides without a bear sighting. But, we knew they were there. Enormous paw prints and scat littered the River's edge.

Black Bear with her two Kermode Cubs

After helicopter pilot Chad Friesen lifted off King Pacific's Lodge dock, the 30-minute flight took us skimming over rugged peaks topped with glacial lakes then swooshing through narrow valleys. Pat Werner, her husband Bill, and I talked through our headset intercom of our anticipation of a day of heli-fishing, and the probability of seeing grizzlies, a species not found on Princess Royale Island, the location of the lodge. While black bear and the rare Kermode, also known as the spirit bear, a recessive gene black bear are frequent sightings during Lodge adventures, the grizzly is known to only inhabit the mainland of British Columbia.

The Bell 206 Jet Ranger set down on the beach next to the Khutz River, Tsimshian for "long inlet in a steep valley," located on British Columbia's mainland. Without shutting off his engine, Friesen lifted off as we turned our backs to a backwash of flying sand. We had arranged a pick up for mid-afternoon. The four of us were now totally alone in the wilderness of the Great Bear Rainforest.

That wonderful "mood of the mountain" offered fog banked crevices with steam rising from wet sandy areas on the beach. Closer to the river, the cobblestone beach was covered with rocks and boulders of various sizes. The River's crystal green and blue glacial water provided great visibility of numerous schools of pink salmon migrating upriver to spawn.

Spawning salmon, including pink, chum, and Coho, the latter whom hang in the deeper, more protected water eddies of the Khutz, stop feeding when they enter a river system from the Pacific. Focused on surviving until they spawn, they become very "territorial". A colorful pink showgirl streamer angers them, and they strike furiously whenever a fly is presented.

Once salmon enter a river, their bodies soften, scar, and begin to deteriorate, and the jaw of the male becomes hooked. Even better tasting salmon, like Chinook and Coho, are released to complete their spawning, die, and enter the food chain, primarily as the prey of bear, wolf, eagles, and gulls.

The water's clarity and the sunny day made it easy to spot schools of fish making this final upstream struggle. The gentle flow of the water and a sandy bottom made the wading easy. The fish seemed oblivious to our presence or the quality of fly presentation. While casting in those conditions might be easy, the catching was another story. The fish averaged about 6-10 pounds, and with an 8-weight rod, they put up a decent fight. The challenge was one of not snagging a fish that might take a while running in circles around your legs. It was cast, hook up, fight, and release…one fish after another, all day long. That is the reason Pat took a break next to the log.

After three hours of fighting fish, Logan suggested that we stop to "pecker", or take a break to enjoy a picnic lunch. Retrieving our food, cached in a tree, we munched hungrily as we pondered paw prints in the sand.

Long before we could see it, the echo of the helicopter's rotor bounced off cliff walls. The day had passed all too quickly. How rare are those days when everything is perfect, including the weather and the fishing, plus the added excitement of grizzly bear encounters?

A Mary L. Peachin Adventure

During fall spawning season, Pilot Paul Tosczak skimmed the bright red Bell 260 helicopter just above the treetops over the Quall River inlet so we could search fall's crystal clear water for pink salmon. Spotting a school making their way upstream, Paul hovered then lowered the 4-passenger helicopter gently into a green meadow filled with colorful summer flowers.

Hopping out the rotor spinning, Guide Wayne Boles assembled two 8-weight fly rods with pink showgirls, a feathery fly that resembles a leech when soaked in the current. Fellow angler and photographer Carl Duncan and I walked the short distance from the meadow to wade into the river.

"These fish aren't interested in feeding. They are on a mission!" Wayne continued, "They'll go for that flash of pink on the fly whenever it is placed in front of them." Sure enough, on the first cast I hooked into a 6-pounder, sea lice still attached to its tail. He told me, "This fish just entered the river from its ocean journey; lice don't live long in fresh water."

The clear water of the Quall enabled me to watch the salmon and brightness of the fly zip through the water. As I waded waist deep along the river's sandy bottom, the salmon swam in circles around my feet, I followed them with the tip of the rod.

A thunderous sound echoed off the canyon wall. I wondered if a storm could interrupt this glorious sunny day. "Oh, no", Wayne explained, "That's just another avalanche caused by melting snow on the higher peaks of the Coastal range."

As we continued to hook into fish, Wayne noticed clumps of grass floating in the current. "There is a bear upstream." Having listened to his bear safety lecture ("give them their space and back up"), I queried as to whether he had brought a gun. "No, this time of year they are interested in berries, but as more salmon enter the stream, this place will be loaded with bear."

Nearby, we could hear an owl hooting above the ripple of the current. When we had fished out the pool, Wayne suggested we move on. Thinking we would be wading upstream, Wayne pointed me toward the helicopter, and once again we lifted off. After passing over the bear grazing upstream, we again began our aerial scouting.

The day went quickly and as the sun began to drop behind the snow-capped peaks, our departure was expedited when Carl and Paul spotted a black bear headed our way. We gave him his fishing hole back as we headed back to the Lodge.

On the return flight, Wayne pointed out lakes they drop into to fish for trout. The isolation of Lowe and Klewnuggett lakes make them only accessible by helicopter. With no competition from other anglers, they yield countless releases of native cutthroat and rainbow.

The scenic 15- to 30-minute flight passed over breathless fiords and inlets. After a day of heli-fishing, it's hard to imagine wading side by side with other anglers try to hook angler-savvy fish. This is an ultimate fly fishing experience.

Great Bear Rainforest

Twice the size of Yellowstone National Park, the Great Bear Rainforest encompasses 4.4 million acres. Covering almost 2/3 or 250 miles of British Columbia's central coastline, the isolated temperate Rainforest is accessible only by float plane or boat. Noted for its 1,000-year-old 300-foot red cedar, western hemlock, Douglas fir and 100-foot Sitka spruce, the 25,000-square-mile forest has more than 2,500 salmon runs, fish who returned to the rivers of their birth. It is also habitat for the Pacific's southernmost coastal grizzly population. The unique salmon, bear, and forest ecosystem sustain its healthy environment.

The Great Bear Rainforest, one of the largest unspoiled temperate rainforests, was established in February 2006 by an agreement between British Columbia's provincial government and a coalition of conservationists, loggers, hunters, and First Nations people. The agreement ensured a plan of protection and forest management.

Home to hundreds of species, including cougars, wolves, grizzlies, black, and Kermode spirit bears, the Great Bear Rainforest's biological abundance is the result of 10,000 years of evolution dating back to a time when glaciers of the Pleistocene Epoch melted. The proximity of the ocean to the mountains provides a warm offshore flow creating an abundance of precipitation over mountain ranges, a phenomenon that creates its lush forest.

From the northern coast of Vancouver Island to the Alaskan border, the Great Bear Rainforest is the ancestral home of nearly a dozen First Nations bands. Approximately 30,000 people live in small village or reserves, and as guardians of the land, they care and live on its abundance.

Rare Kermode Bear: Photo Credit Joyce Follman

Westcoast Milbanke Sound Lodge

Milbanke, the third of Westcoast Fishing Resort's (WCF) three lodges, is known for more than just angling. Surrounded by old growth forest, eagles fly while orcas play in the Sound's tranquil waters, ones that are packed with chinook and coho salmon until the fall.

The Resorts have a simple dining philosophy: use the finest ingredients available and prepare with care. The rest takes care of itself. They feel that their galleys are there for the angler's relaxation and enjoyment with friends.

Breakfast includes a variety of continental items as well as a hot breakfast buffet. Anglers wishing a more leisurely approach to the fishing day can take time for daily specials as well as eggs any style. A table full of goodies awaits the angler to pack for the boat along with sandwiches, soda, or beer.

Lunch is a hot buffet featuring a menu of burgers and fish and chips and a full line up of fresh salads, soups, and other items. If the salmon bite is just too good to make the trip back to the lodge, they offer hot lunch on the water as well.

Dinner is the time to relax and share the day's stories (and lies) accompanied by some of the Pacific Northwest's finest offerings both in food and drink. The 3-course service is served with complementary wine. Aperitifs and coffee accompany the Pastry Chef's nightly creations.

Westcoast Resort's Fishing Instructor Program has been designed for all ages and skill levels. A comprehensive orientation session allows even the most novice angler to quickly become familiar with safe vessel operation. Their boats' safety and navigational equipment have the quality, if necessary, to withstand the rigors of their remote locations.

Friendly and experienced WCR guides instruct guests on local fishing techniques and the lodge's current "hot spots". All fishing and premium foul-weather gear is provided; guests may also choose to bring along their own favorite rods and reels.

All packages include five hours of guided fishing instruction with the option to upgrade to a guide for 10 hours per day if booked in advance. Anglers may also opt to fish entirely on their own. This option limits allowable time on the water to daylight hours, as Westcoast Resort's commitment is to provide a safe, supervised on-water experience.

Any catch brought to the deck will be prepared by the skilled dock crew who will take fillet, vacuum pack, and flash freeze your fish. Additional options include custom fish processing: canned, smoked, or candied.

(Source Westcoast Fishing Resorts)

www.westcoastresorts.com

A Mary L. Peachin Adventure

SALMON ON! An angler, easily distracted by the striking beauty of British Columbia's old growth rainforests, deserted beaches, or gushing waterfalls, can easily miss the bite, that quick snap of the salmon pulling the trolling line out of a downrigger.

Fishing at Westcoast Resorts' Whale Channel's 23-room floating lodge is "uncrowded, untouched, and unbelievable". Its best fishing spots are less than a 5-minute boat ride. Sheltering islands protect anglers from dealing with the ordeal of rockin' and rolling in ocean swells.

Brad "Ripper" Clarke, who guided for 10 years at Whale Channel shared, "50,000 Chinook (king) salmon pass Whale Channel as they head north 60 miles to their spawning river, one that empties into Douglas Channel near the town of Kitimat. They are stronger and fight harder than any other salmon I have caught."

A good day on the water for head guide Brent "Brentos" Gill is a "grand slam: catching a tyee (a salmon weighing more than 30 pounds), watching orcas, and seeing humpback whales feed, while eagles soar overhead."

Two out of Westcoast Resorts five lodges follow the salmon migration, until recent years where they have remained solely at Milbanke Sound. At the time of my visit, Whale Channel welcomed schooling fish in late May near the banks of remote (90 miles south of Prince Rupert) Barnard Harbour. In mid-July, Westcoast Fishing cast the cables anchoring the lodge to the shore to "follow the fish" down the Inside Passage where calmer waters and Alaskan cruise ships motored, to the isolated, secluded Louisa Cove on Wurtele Island. Whale Channel lodge morphed its name into the lodge at Milbanke Sound, isolated by being 80 miles from civilization, and accessible only by seaplane or boat. Today, the lodge remains and is called Milbanke Sound.

It was a tremendous effort, one that is not missed. Moving a lodge built on a 165 x 50 feet steel barge isn't all in a day's work. Preparation includes securing anything that might break from motion encountered while undertow. Within six hours of the last guests' departure, a tugboat pulls the lodge southward. While it may only be 70 miles as the eagle flies, a calmer 120-mile route is tracked to avoid open ocean swells. Provided that weather conditions are good, the tow job takes about 24 hours. The crew has two days after arriving in

Milbanke Sound to get things in order before the first guests arrive. Permanent docks in each location help to expedite the relocation.

Westcoast Resorts believe guests should experience remote, unspoiled areas of British Columbia's coastline without the crowds. While most anglers have their heart set on returning home with salmon for the barbeque, others might want to forego some of their valuable fishing time to enjoy the lodge's amenities.

After a day's fishing, there are choices: soak in the open air hot tub surrounded by 360 degree views of the ocean, allow the massage therapist to perform her magic on tired muscles, or stretch them out with a run on the treadmill or lifting free weights in the workout facility. Some might want to relax by shooting a game of pool or just heading to the Liar's lounge to listen to the day's stories unfold.

In a cedar and glass-walled dining room, breakfast is a buffet unless the angler would rather to dally with made-to-order requests. An angler who wants to fish all day can grab a sandwich, beverages, and a cookie from the "shepherd boat", one that restocks anglers with bait and tackle, instead of heading back to the lodge for a delicious lunch buffet. Dinner is a 3-course gourmet meal with a choice of entrée, served with premium wines.

Northern British Columbia's landscape is stunning. A pod of mighty killer whales might pass by the boat while humpbacks playfully breech or spy hop. Stellar sea lions lounge on a nearby rock outcropping. The rare sighting of a kermode or spirit bears, indigenous to the surrounding rainforest, is possible. Seeing a grizzly or black bear prowling the beaches during low tide to dig for clams is more likely.

Milbanke Sound offers several charitable events and tournaments. two weekends are billed as a "couples retreat". Being the more serious angler, my husband questioned, "Is this event going to be marriage counseling or a swinging affair?" No, I enticed, it's a romantic couples' weekend fishing trip to an idyllic place, with "lots of food and wine".

For the past three seasons, WestCoast Resorts has offered salmon fishing weekends for spouses. Daily wine tasting, held in the courtyard of the lodge, provides an opportunity to learn about wines from renowned Okanagan vintners like Quail's Gate estate, Grey Monk, Sumac Ridge, and Hawthorne. A weekend highlight is a 6-course winemaker's gourmet dinner prepared by Executive Chef Glenn Gatske. In Liar's Lounge, where anglers usually share fish tales, a duo plays romantic background music and classical favorites. It's an opportunity to "Fish, laugh, and fall in love all over again!"

Whale Channel, and Milbanke Sound, offers the angler a moveable feast. They can dine on the flaky pink meat of a Chinook on the floating lodge and have their catch flash frozen to take home for a memorable winter's barbecue. (Featured in *Robb Report*)

Westwind Tugboat Adventures

Westwind Tugboat offers mobile wilderness fishing by anchoring at Haida Gwaii's Langara Island, then following the salmon through Inside Passage channels, between the coastal mountains Prince Rupert and the Cariboo Chilcotin coastal region of Bella Bella.

The 1941 vintage tugboat offers saltwater and stream fishing with an abundance of variety in landscape and wildlife. There's time to go ashore for clam digging, crabbing, explore on nature hikes, beachcomb, or whale watch.

Carrying a maximum of 12 guests allows personal service and friendship. The tugboat, which serves as a base, provides two per person fully equipped, self-guided 18-foot fishing skiffs to fish, explore or relax.

Each tugboat has an experienced fish guide, always on the fishing grounds, who shares his time with all guests.

Westwind Tugboat considers the world famous Langara fishery unsurpassed. Along the northwest tip of Haida Gwaii Islands they fish for Chinook as well as halibut and ling cod. Prince Rupert, British Columbia's undiscovered northern hot spot bordering the Alaska panhandle, is home to Skeena and Nass Rivers salmon runs.

Anglers fishing in the Cariboo Chilcotin Coast region of Bella Bella can take advantage of calm water channels allowing access to river estuaries and bays teeming with salmon.

A Westwind Tugboat Adventure is a great family vacation. The heritage wooden tugboats are well maintained with well-appointed two berth cabins, a fireside lounge, bathrooms and showers, plus a busy galley serving unbelievable food and desserts. Anglers are provided with bathrobes, extra pillows, and a complimentary selection of international wines. Onboard, the skipper and crew are eager to pamper you and the shipboard atmosphere is totally relaxing.

(Source: Westwind Tugboat)

www.tugboatcruise.com

Rivers Inlet

Introduction

This Central Coast 28 mile (45K) fjord is located 40 miles (65k) north of Vancouver Island, south of Hakai Pass, the entrance to Queen Charlotte Strait, and 78 miles (125 k) southwest of Bella Coola.

Fitz Hugh Sound is the entrance to its primary community of the same name. The logging and fishing town is home of the Wuikinuxv. Rivers feeding Rivers Inlet are the Kilbella River and its tributary, the Chuckwalla, and the Wannock River, which feeds the head of Rivers Inlet and is fed by the fresh-water fjord Owikeno Lake. Within the inlet, about nine miles (15k) is Moses Inlet, which is fed by the Clyak River.

Rivers Inlet was named by George Vancouver for George Pitt, 1st Baron Rivers (1721-1803). Two of his men, Peter Puget and Joseph Whidbey, were the first to chart it in 1792.

Black Gold Lodge

Since 1988, Black Gold Lodge at Rivers Inlet has been a premiere sport-fishing destination along British Columbia's rugged central Pacific coast. Anglers stay in comfortable, well-appointed cabins while they enjoy the Lodge service from experienced staff.

Rivers Inlet is considered one of British Columbia's scenic and unspoiled places. Located 300 miles north of Vancouver with the nearest road 80 miles away, it is accessible by boat or seaplane. The area, rich with wildlife, includes bald eagles, orcas, river otters, cougars, bears, sea lions, and other species. Close-up whale encounters are frequent, sometimes as near as the window of the Lodge.

Some of British Columbia's largest salmon congregate in Rivers Inlet en route to spawning grounds in three major river systems. Adding to anglers' pleasure is when they are still actively feeding prior on this final leg of their journey. Black Gold Lodge boasts that more 50-60-pound Chinook are recorded in its 30-mile fjord than any other provincial fishery.

It's all about location, and Black Gold being at the mouth of the Inlet provides a longer period of productive fishing. Travel in larger boats to other fishing areas is not required.

The Lodge offers an "All Inclusive" option featuring gourmet meals with beer or wine, boat upgrades, and other premium services including return airfare from Vancouver, a deluxe private cabins with bedroom, sitting area, and bathroom for two or more anglers, and a self-serve sandwich and snack bar between 5:00 AM and 10:00 PM. Also included is a fishing instruction seminar with guiding by the fish master to Rivers Inlet most productive fishing grounds, custom cleaning and vacuuming packaging of fish, the use of 16 or 17 aluminum Hourstoncrafts with two swivel seats and a 15 horsepower motor. They are equipped with a depth sounder, radio, compass, area charts, and all safety flotation and water safety necessities required by law.

Rods, reels, bait, and terminal tackle or lures and jigs can be either brought to the Lodge or purchased in the gift shop. There is access to Internet, telephone, and satellite television. Raingear and even loaner suits for the hot tub are available.

While Black Gold pride themselves on exceptional service, they make it a point not to interfere with the fishing experience. Anglers keep their own schedule, fishing from morning through evening.

When the bite's on, the last thing an angler wants is to have to return to the Lodge for more bait or supplies. With just a radio call to the tackle shop, they'll bring you whatever fishing equipment or bait you might need. If they hear reports of action in another location, they'll let you know. After fishing, dock hands will clean and refuel your boat, check your equipment, and restock your tackle box.

For anyone new to salmon fishing, or wanting a refresher, Black Gold offers a fishing clinic during the afternoon of the first fishing day. They explain everything from operating the boat, baiting the hook, proper techniques for setting the hook, playing a big fish, and boat-side netting. The fish master will escort you on your first trip to the famous Wall, a consistent producer of big fish. Your tackle box includes a detailed fishing map showing many other great fishing areas.

Those anglers not taking advantage of the "All Inclusive" offer will pay for their meals, airfare, fishing license, raingear, plus gratuities. There is no charge for children under 12 with two paying adults.

(Source: Black Gold Lodge)

www.blackgoldlodge.com

Duncanby Lodge

Rivers Inlet Duncanby Lodge's primary mission is the operation of a fishing lodge. But they value the time to marvel at an angler's opportunity to view a spectacular landscape including 28 (40K) miles of ocean and mountains leading to the headwaters of the Wannock and Kilbella Rivers.

Some of these tours include a motor to the head of Drainy Inlet, a place some guides call Jurassic park, or exploring serene Moses inlet to the mouth of the untouched Clyak River. There are pods of humpback whales, plus the falls in Waterfall Inlet. Fishing attracts anglers to Rivers Inlet, but the environment is the lure that brings them back.

Rivers Inlet is home to a diverse recreational fishery. Fishing grounds vary from large bull kelp beds to deep-water ocean to river estuaries holding multiple fish species. These conditions provide anglers the option to use a variety of fishing techniques: mooching, trolling, jigging, spin casting, and fly fishing. Duncanby Lodge has kayaks and canoes available for bear viewing or bird watching dominated by bald eagles and loons.

A stay at the Lodge includes all the necessary gear required. Anglers can choose to fish unguided or use the expertise of a guide. Duncanby Lodge's team of seven professional guides is ready to ensure anglers maximize time to experience the Duncanby difference. Advance reservations are recommended for guide services.

Fully guided days include fishing the best tides for either 12 hours or half days of six hours. Duncanby offers seven full time guides, a fleet of a dozen 22- to 28-foot Grady White boats, and a non-guided fleet of open center console designed Boston Whalers and Hourston Glasscraft.

Unguided anglers using the Hurston Glasscraft have a comfortable ride with retractable convertible top for sunny or rainy days. These boats, lighter than the Whalers, are equipped with a 50 HP Yamaha 4-stroke outboard engines.

At the end of the fishing day, dock staff assists in parking and unloading catch. Boats are meticulously detailed, pressure washed, then restocked for the following day. All boats are outfitted with a Garmin GPS, depth sounder, VHF radio, Scotty downriggers, rods, a tackle box with mooching gear, fresh towels, net, gaff, Lodge map, and safety equipment.

Anglers are offered preferred rates, shuttle service, and fish freezer and storage capabilities at their choice of Pacific Gateway Hotel Vancouver

Airport, River Rock Casino Resort, or Marriott Vancouver Airport Hotel. Seair floatplanes provide a Cessna Caravan charter hour plus flight from Vancouver to the Lodge.

(Source: Duncanby Lodge)

www.duncanbylodgemarina.com

River's Inlet Legacy Lodge

Known for its magnificent scenery and unparalleled salmon fishing, the waters of Rivers Inlet hold some of British Columbia's largest Chinook and coho salmon. More Chinook, in the 50-60 pound range, are caught yearly in this fjord-like inlet. Full of energy and fight, these salmon can battle for hours, covering incredible distances.

Rivers Inlet lies within the Great Bear Rainforest, a unique expanse of coastal temperate rainforest. Larger than eight-million acres, it is five times the size of Banff National Park and represents one of the world's most diverse ecosystems.

Rivers Inlet holds the largest concentration of brown bears in British Columbia. With more than 20 streams, rivers, and feeder creeks supporting the annual spawning rituals of all five salmon species, it represents the epicenter of the province's salmon producing areas.

Rivers Inlet's long history of commercial fishing and canneries has given way to attracting an adventurous angler who searches its craggy shoreline and steep granite walls for North America's largest salmon, the Wannock River Chinook.

Abundant coho, some exceeding 20 pounds, migrate close to the water's surface. They can be so aggressive that they are often caught a few feet behind the boat. The experience of having a 20-pound coho strike your cut plug bait trolled so close from your rod tip then, within seconds, peeling 200 feet of line off your single action reel is the definition of Rivers Inlet Legacy Lodge's excitement.

Fertile waters offer a variety of bottom feeders including halibut, yellow eye and lingcod. Legacy Lodge offers exceptional saltwater fly fishing for Pacific salmon on the Inlet's calm, protected waters. Anglers of all abilities can enjoy fishing large Northern coho on 8-weight Sage fly rods and reels, all equipped with the best sinking and floating lines and productive flies. Salmon can be taken on a casted fly or by bucktailing along the shorelines of Rivers Inlet.

Bucktailing is an exciting way to catch salmon on light fly gear without requiring challenging casting techniques. Bucktailing also allows the more experienced angler to "cover more ground" while searching for the fish.

Scout boats provide easier access to dense populations of large Northern coho and Chinook inhabiting shoals, leading points and kelp beds near the shorelines of Rivers Inlet.

Legacy Lodge's high-performance Scout 175 boats are equipped with Yamaha 70 HP 4-stroke smokeless outboards, a Lowrance Gen2 HDS–7 Fish Finder, VHF radios, GPS, premium tackle and gear, plus fuel and bait. They have a center console with large, dry fish and tackle storage. The Lodge provides rain suits, rubber boots, personal flotation devices (PFD), and professional instruction on local fishing techniques. Scout 175 sport fishing boats allow anglers to fish anywhere in Rivers Inlet, a place where only whales can interrupt the adventure.

The polished Sport boat delivers a vast array of fishing features, including a 94-quart removable cooler/seat with backrest, extensive bow casting platform with separate storage area, aerated live well and plenty of seating and rod holders. A 10-foot draft provides unknown fishing spots to your itinerary.

Legacy Lodge offers three distinct fishing seasons. Traditional salmon fishing (mooching) and fly fishing for Chinook and coho salmon is available from July through September in secluded locations throughout Rivers Inlet. Halibut, Yellow Eye, and Lingcod are plentiful all summer. Heli-fishing for huge Northern coho salmon (20-plus lbs) along pristine coastline rivers is available during September and October, and wild steelhead fishing from helicopters is available during April and May.

The Legacy Lodge guides and instructors program is based on personal service and differs as they provide in-boat instruction on a 2-3 hour rotating basis. This allows those familiar with mooching to fish on their own as much as desired while having the benefit of a guide's knowledge of the waters, techniques, and premier fishing locations. For the individuals new to salmon fishing, guides create success for all anglers by accelerating the learning curve and providing in-boat assistance throughout their trip. The team leads daily halibut fishing excursions within the same calm waters, assisting guests with the use of the GPS and effective halibut techniques.

The goal is to provide our guests with expert assistance while still allowing them to have the freedom to explore and create their own adventure. Unlike other experiences, Legacy Lodge takes pride in providing a true "fishing adventure of a lifetime".

All meals prepared by Executive Chef Courtney Burnham feature traditional Pacific Northwest local ingredients with a menu of fresh seafood, native delicacies, and prime beef. Breakfast is prepared before a day of fishing with a selection of hot or cold drinks and snacks on board and waiting for the angler's departure. Breakfast sandwiches, hot coffee, snacks, and lunch are also delivered daily to anglers on the water.

Legacy Lodge, overlooking Pendelton Bay, is an awakening to nature for those who yearn for the perfect fishing vacation. Their experienced guides have fished the waters of the Pacific Northwest, from Oregon to Alaska, for more than 20 years. They agree that casting a line at Legacy Lodge can be defined as wild beauty with incredible fishing.

Carved into the rugged coastline approximately 280 nautical miles north of Vancouver, Legacy Lodge sits at the mouth of the famed Rivers Inlet. This fjord-like inlet is 38 miles long and its mouth is seven miles wide.

Travel to the Lodge is a one hour chartered flight from Vancouver International Airport's South Terminal to Port Hardy, located on the northern tip of Vancouver Island. A scenic 30-minute flight by seaplane crosses Queen Charlotte Sound to Legacy Lodge. This flight over the British Columbia coast is spectacular and a great photo opportunity. The fishing package includes round-trip airfare from Vancouver's South Terminal to the Lodge as well as deluxe accommodations. These include all meals, like hot lunches served on the water and incredible Pacific Northwest cuisine served with wine for dinner. Also included in the package is daily use of fully equipped, custom-designed Scout boats, four on-water Instructors, the finest in fishing gear, plus all the fuel and bait you need. In addition, professional fish handling (cleaned, vacuum-packed, and frozen) of your catch is provided for your trip home. All fish are shipped in insulated cardboard boxes acceptable to all major airlines.

(Source: Legacy Lodge)

www.legacylodge.com

Rivers Inlet Sportsman's Club

Rivers Inlet Sportsman's Club, 300 miles north of Vancouver, is accessible only by floatplane. No roads, no crowds. Recognized as a place where record Chinook return each year to feed and spawn, Rivers Inlet holds the record for British Columbia's largest Chinook salmon. In recent years salmon weighing over 70 pounds have been caught, trophy coho also return each summer providing non-stop fishing action.

The Sportsman's Club is a floating lodge nestled in a tranquil bay, only minutes from the world famous BC salmon fishing spot, "The Wall".

The Club's facilities are ideal for everyone. It is a place where friends and family can spend uninterrupted quality time together or corporate groups can have an intimate venue to facilitate memorable relations with clients and customers.

The Rivers Inlet Sportsman's Club prides itself in offering intimacy, isolation, exceptional service, first-class equipment, spectacular scenery, whale watching, and wildlife viewing in a remote wilderness setting.

Accommodations include cabins on top of a series of inter-locking floating docks. Each cedar room has two double beds with a private bathroom and entrance. All rooms are double-occupancy with several triple-occupancy rooms available for groups with odd numbers. Their commitment to cleanliness is evident throughout the lodge. Each evening turn-down service comes complete with chocolate and a hot water bottle to ensure a warm bed when you retire for the evening.

Gourmet meals ensure that the angler is never hungry. Three buffet style meals are served so there is choice for individual tastes. Fresh made soups, salads, and breads are served with lunch and dinner. A box lunch can be arranged if you plan to travel some distance to fish or prefer to stay out on the water. The close proximity of Rivers Inlet Sportsman's Club to the fishing grounds typically results in anglers stopping for a hot lunch, or taking a break to re-provision.

In addition to the three meals served, boat snacks are provided and a hot snack is served in the lounge every evening after fishing. Between fishing sessions or after a full day on the water anglers enjoy relaxing in the comfortable lounge where they can watch guides process the days catch at the nearby cleaning table, mingle with the other guests, exchange stories of the day's adventures, or play a game of cards or chess.

The bar is fully stocked with juices, soft drinks, coffee, tea, hot chocolate, and condiments for all types of drinks. Spirits and beer can be ordered at British Columbia liquor store prices. They label bottle and leave them at the bar for your convenience.

Rivers Inlet Sportsman's Club salmon fishing technique is called "motor mooching." The angler lowers the line to shallow depths of five to twenty-five feet. By moving the motor in and out of gear the angler varies the depth and action of the slowly rolling herring. The Club has found this the most productive method for fishing Chinook. They have found that larger salmon like to linger away from the current close to shore among the rocks and kelp. The cut plug herring imitates a "wounded bait fish," one that is easy prey for these lazy salmon.

They use a trolling technique for fishing for coho. The angler keeps the engine in gear so the bait imitates a livelier baitfish. Coho like a more vigorous baitfish and tend to school further off shore typically between 10 to 300 yards.

On stormy days, if a swell enters the Inlet, a series of islands in front of our fishing lodge offer further protection. There is always a calm place to fish in Rivers Inlet. Their premier salmon fishing spot, "The Wall", is only five minutes from the dock. This proximity allows our guests to conveniently return to the fishing lodge. There are also many other fishing grounds within a 3-30-minute boat ride from the fishing lodge. Guest can always find an isolated fishing spot to call their own.

Halibut fishing and lingcod fishing hot spots are also an equal distance from the lodge. A day on the water with one of their fishing experts will accelerate your knowledge, improve your local expertise, and increase your chances of landing the "big one". All Rivers Inlet Sportsman's Club guides are extensively trained for British Columbia salmon fishing in Rivers Inlet, and many have worked on their docks for several years. Guiding at Rivers Inlet Sportsman's Club can be customized to your own needs. Anglers may pre-book guides, which are rotated, for a single day or their entire trip. There is always a fish master on the water to assist anglers at all times, someone nearby to answer questions, re-stock your bait and refreshments, and to ensure your safety.

In addition to great salmon fishing there are other experiences to enjoy in the remote wilderness location. Some options include a walk through the temperate rainforest or beachcombing a rarely explored white sand beach, salmon fishing from a kayak, or exploring many coves and bays in a double ocean kayaks, row boat, or paddle boat, or just photographing whales, seals and eagles for amazing wild life photography. There is much to see and do in remote Rivers Inlet.

Boats are custom crafted 17-foot fiberglass vessels designed for safety, comfort, and fishing stability. They are open with no center console or windshield to get in the way while fighting fish. Boats are powered by 40 HP 4-stroke Yamaha outboards.

All equipment is provided. If you have a specialty reel or rod, feel free to bring it. The Club provides 10 ½-foot mooching rods with 2-8 ounce weights, 25-pound test line, and either single or multi-action reels. For added excitement they provide light tackle fly rods fitted with 12-pound test line or traditional fly fishing tackle. For bottom fishing they use multi action reels with one-pound weight, spreader bars, and 100-pound fire-wire braided line. Bass masters will enjoy non-stop action when fishing with spin casting rods for rock cod and ling cod in the kelp beds.

If the weather takes a turn, comfortable raingear and boots are provided to keep the angler dry from head to foot.

Transportation from Vancouver's South Airport Terminal is by Seair Seaplanes.

(Source: Rivers Inlet Sportsman's Club)
www.riversinlet.com

Fly Fishing Destinations

Introduction

Lower Dean Fly Fishery

The Dean River, a coastal British Columbia wilderness river, is one considered to rank as one yielding finest summer steelhead run.

The mouth of the Dean flows as a small stream from Nimpo Lake. Meandering slowly to the northwest into nearby Anahim Lake, it flows past Abuntlet and Lessard Lake towards Tweedsmuir Provincial Park. This upper area is accessible by boat and best known for wild rainbow trout. Services and facilities, which include resorts and lodges, can be found in the nearby communities of Nimpo and Anahim Lake.

In Tweedsmuir Park, the Dean River turns west, travelling downward through the Coast mountain range to the Dean Channel and out into the Pacific Ocean. The lower portion of the Dean, from the mouth of the river to Crag Creek, is the salmon and steelhead section. It can only be reached by boat via Dean Channel or by air.

Hodson's Dean River Lodge

Bud Hodson, an early Dean River steelhead pioneer and founder of the family operation, passed the torch to his son Danny, and his grandsons now run and guide on this legendary river.

In addition to their main camp, Hodson's Lodge has a rustic steelhead camp located 25 miles upstream of the main lodge. During the heart of the summer season, anglers visiting Hodson's Lodge will spend several days at the upper camp. Danny Hodson typically flies them there by helicopter. That upper camp section of the River is considered some of the finest for trophy steelhead dry fly water.

Cabins sleep two anglers. They are equipped with propane lights, a wood stove, and cold running water. When the camp generator is running, electricity is available in the cabins. Hodson's main lodge contains shower facilities, a dining room, and lounge. Hearty home-style meals are served family-style.

The Dean River is famous for its aggressive summer run steelhead. Anglers are accompanied by knowledgeable guides and transported by jet boats. Dean River steelhead range in size from 8- 20 pounds, with the average steelhead weighing between 10 and 12 pounds. Hodson's Lodge runs three steelhead anglers per boat on the Lower Dean River with two anglers per boat at their Upper Camp. In total, they are able to access over 20 miles of fishable water.

During the warmer temperatures and longer daylight hours of July and August, Hodson's Lodge operates on a "split" schedule. A steelhead angler's day begins with a daylight breakfast. Coffee and cookies are sent out on the river for a mid-morning break and anglers return to the lodge at noon for a main meal. Fishing resumes around 4:00 PM. Guides will provide supper over a campfire. Remaining on the river until dusk, anglers returning to camp 10:00 PM.

In September, a full day of fishing is offered with anglers spending the day on the river with a hot lunch streamside before returning to the lodge for an early evening meal.

Hodson's main lodge is located seven miles from Dean Channel saltwater on the north side of the Dean River. Upper Camp is located 25 miles from the saltwater and is accessed by a 10-minute helicopter flight. A guest cabin and lodge with shower facilities and dining room compliment this remote fishing experience. The Dean River flows into the Dean Channel on the central British Columbian coast just north of Bella Coola.

(Source: Hodson's Lodge)
www.flywatertravel.com

Kimsquit Bay Lodge

The Lodge, located above Kimsquit Bay's turquoise waters, has sweeping views of glaciated, snow-capped Coastal mountains rising high above Dean Channel. The thundering roar of adjacent Grantham Falls stirs the air. The Lodge's location is positioned to target steelhead: close to the Pacific, located in the lower River, below the turbulent white water of the lower Dean River Canyon. It is a comfortable, intimate, family-style lodge. Anglers are accommodated in six double-occupancy cabins, each with their own private bathroom. A home-style dining room and comfortable lounge adds to the charm. They appreciate good food and serve fresh, nutritious meals prepared and plated by their chef.

The water they fish is storied and classic from the river's mouth salt chuck of the Dean Channel to the entrance of raging Dean River Canyon. Dynamic, steep gradient, classic, boulder strewn, the River is perfect for fly fishing. Favorite targets are runs with names like Instant Backing, Archaeological, Sub-Tidal, Ross Island, Eagles Nest, and the legendary Cuttbank.

Anglers fish in classic hand-made wooden boats, a 2-toned blue Dean River style dory with 35 HP outboard jet drive. Two guides, who know the River well, specialize in 2-handed spey casting instruction.

A turbine Otter float plane lands on the bay directly in front of the lodge. During the season, the hour charter flight departs on Friday afternoon from Smithers. Anglers are responsible for their transportation from Smithers in northern British Columbia.

(Source Kimsquit Bay Lodge)

www.kimsquitbay.com

Lower Dean River Lodge

Twenty river miles above Dean River Canyon, Lower Dean River Lodge operates two steelhead fly fishing lodges. Their Main Camp, in operation since 1962, accommodates nine guests. Located approximately eight miles from salt water, its dozen buildings include six two-person wooden floored tents with plumbing, a central dining and socializing facility, a double shower house with indoor plumbing, a walk-in cooler, and a generator building to provide electricity. From Main Camp, anglers fly fish 12-14 miles above Dean River Canyon, located two miles from the river mouth.

Upper Camp, operated since 1972, accommodates three anglers and is approximately 17 miles from salt water. It has four buildings and includes a hot shower and electricity. From Upper Camp anglers fly fish five upper miles of river in water that is navigable by boat.

Both camps are fully staffed with an angler ratio of 3:2. Meals are prepared using fresh food flown in weekly. Breakfast and supper are served family style in the lodge.

The Dean River begins as a small stream high in the swamps of the Chilcotin plateau. It flows north through the well-known blue ribbon rainbow trout fishing area, surrounding Nimpo and Anahim Lakes, before turning westward at Anahim Peak to begin its descent towards the Pacific Ocean. Between June and September, the large concentration of summer run steelhead in the lower reaches of the river are held by natural barriers.

A canyon near the mouth of the river keeps weaker salmon out of the system. Only steelhead, Chinook, and coho get through in significant numbers. Chinook enter the river during June and July; coho, up to 20 pounds, arrive between late August and September.

Dean River steelhead enter the river in June then continue to run in waves throughout the season. The average fish is 10-12 pounds with some weighing as much as 25-30 pounds. Steelhead readily take a fly from mid-June spring runoff to the conclusion of fishing season on September 30th. Steelhead fishing is catch and release only.

Chinook, which have been caught weighing up to 60 pounds, enter the River in June and July. These powerful wild salmon can be caught on flies and are a challenging quarry in the fast flowing Dean.

Fly rods should be 7-9-weight, with 8-weight being the most popular. Reels should be sturdy with enough drag to avoid being stripped and hold a 100 yards of 20-pound Dacron backing. Favorite floating lines are fast-sinking with weight forward. It is recommended to bring two rods with an extra spool.

The lodge sells a selection of popular dry and wet patterned flies. Hook sizes range from 1/0-4 for wet flies or 4-8 for dries. Streamers, red, black, or a combination of both colors, are the most attractive wet flies. Popular dries are heavily dressed for flotation and visibility in all sorts of patterns and colors or natural. Steelhead do not actively feed in the river so they are typically not attracted to specific patterns. They are more inclined to react to novelty in terms of color and size.

Travel to the Lower Dean River Lodge begins at Vancouver International Airport's South Terminal. Anglers fly in a Northern Thunderbird Air's pressurized "Beech 1900D" charter to Bella Coola. This approximately one hour flight is over some of British Columbia's most spectacular mountain scenery. Arriving at the Bella Coola Airport anglers are flown 35 minutes to the Lower Dean River Lodge in a West Coast Helicopter's six seat, turbine-powered Eurocopter A-Star.

(Source: Lower Dean River Lodge)

www.lowerdean.com

Skeena River Introduction

The Skeena originates south of the Spatsizi Plateau Wilderness Provincial Park in northwestern British Columbia, forming a divide with the Klappan River, a tributary of the Stikine River. It flows for 350 miles (570 km) before it empties into the Pacific Ocean's Chatham Sound, Telegraph Passage and Ogden Channel.

British Columbia's Skeena River is the 2nd longest river flowing exclusively within the Province. It is important transportation artery, particularly for the Tsimshian and the Gitxsan—whose names translate to "inside the Skeena River" and "people of the Skeena River." During the 1860s Omineca Gold Rush, steamboats operate from the Pacific to Hazelton, the jumping-off point for the trails to the goldfields. The river and its basin sustain a wide variety of fish, wildlife, and vegetation. Communities in the area are dependent on the health of the river.

While the Skeena has salmon migrations, it is unique for its summer run of steelhead.

Skeena River Lodge

Twenty miles outside the city of Terrace, Skeena River Lodge seven acres is in close to proximity more than just the majestic Skeena River. They also fly fish the Kitimat, Copper (Zymoetz), and Kalum (Kitsumkalum).

The rustic handcrafted post and beam cabin, which accommodates 6-

8 anglers, provides the basics to ensure anglers are well rested and fed with comfortable single beds, a hot shower, and wholesome home-cooked meals.

During September and October, the Lodge operates a remote location on the banks of Meziaden Lake close to the Alaskan border. Nass Base Camp, formerly a tent camp, is now a 1,700 square foot log home with an adjacent guide cabin. At this location a maximum of four anglers with two guides can fish the Bell Irving River.

The Skeena River Lodge experience includes providing the angler with knowledge about the fishery, spey and switch single-handed casting instruction, fly selection, sink tip usage, and line control and presentation methods. Their guides will provide you with all the ingredients needed to release a trophy fish. In addition to fishing the elusive steelhead, they fish all five species of salmon.

The scenery along the Skeena is breathtaking. Moose, bear, and wolf can be viewed along with bald eagles soaring near snow-capped mountains. Long days are spent on the river. Many glacial-fed streams, surrounded by pristine forests, become shrouded in fog.

Skeena River Lodge uses custom made jet boats: Outlaws, Wolfmade, Harbercraft and Alumafi, some with Teflon bottoms to get to shallow fishing spots. AIRE self-bailing 10, 12, and 13-foot white water rafts allow them to navigate around large boulders and through rapids.

With rods days along the length of the Skeena, the Lodge also has permits for other fisheries including the Kitimat River, a favorite for its size, shape, and geographic position. The Kitimat offers a spring steelhead run, followed by an impressive Chinook, chum, pink, and short coho run in the summer.

(Source: Skeena River Lodge)

www.skeenariverlodge.com

Skeena Spey Fishing Lodge

Located on the banks of the Skeena River in Terrace, Skeena Spey Fishing Lodge offers fly anglers the opportunity to target large Chinook salmon and steelhead. They offer instructional guided fishing, casting lessons and fly tying lessons for individuals of any experience level.

The peaceful retreat is a series of riverside A-frame cabins. Hot coffee is delivered to your cabin daily followed by a full breakfast prepared by Chef Josh Wolfe. Owner Malcolm Wood operates multiple award-winning restaurants, assuring that anglers will enjoy satisfying meals.

The property has access to complimentary Internet and cell phone reception allows the angler the ability, if necessary, to work in the wilderness.

Guided fly fishing packages range from their popular Quick Trip Package, perfect for a weekend getaway, week long, or a 10-day extended week.

Skeena Spey Fishing Lodge offers premium fishing gear including brands like: Redington, Pieroway Fly Rods, Hatch Outdoors, and Einarsson reels.

You will have access to top quality Redington waders, boots, and wading jackets. Guides operate custom built Skeena River boats and a new Kingfisher Shallow Water Extreme riverboat.

(Source: Skeena Spey Fishing Lodge)

www.skeenaflyfishing.com

Elk River Introduction

Located in southeastern British Columbia, the Elk River flows for 110 miles before entering the Kootenay River. Renowned for dry-fly fishing for Westslope cutthroat, the River flows through the winter ski town of Fernie. During summer months, Fernie attracts fly fishers. The most easterly British Columbia river headwaters at located in the alpine Elk Lakes. The Elk River carves a valley through the Rocky Mountains as it widens into a mid-size nutrient-rich River.

The River has the classic structure of boulder-strewn runs, deep pools, and riffles, with numerous side channels. An angler can expect to fish attractor dry flies while floating or wading these various types of structure.

A Mary L. Peachin Adventure

Fly Fishing in Fernie

Guide Russell Trand commented, "If these aggressive striking fish would JUMP when hooked, the entire angling world would be here." But savvy fly fishers still come to fish Westslope cutthroat primarily because the species provide a thrill by taking a dry fly on the river's surface.

The Elk is a catch and release river, but anglers who come here count the number of fish released sized by the inches. Most anglers are simply thrilled with the challenge of watching these fish take a properly presented fly.

Our first morning, we put in at Sparwood in Trand's Clacka craft fiberglass dory. We would make an 8-mile 8-hour drift taking out next to Garrett's Ready mix plant. Trand's prior experience as a kayaker and rafting guide brings comfort through sections of rapids in the river.

The geography of the Elk offers great natural fish habitat. Its bottom is strewn with boulders, streams trickle into the river, there are plenty of riffles, and fallen logs protruded from the river, a result of landslides from the edges of steep banks. The water is cold with foam-like slower running nutrient drift lines, a place where fish tend to hang out.

While a day on the river might produce dozens of fish, there are days when "fishing is fishing and not catching". These are the days when an angler might get a chance to enjoy the beauty of the Rockies. We took time to sit on a foldable chair on a sandy bank as Trand prepared a buffet lunch that included sandwich fixings, rice salad with sesame seed oil and ginger, fresh fruit, and homemade dessert. But it's hard to dawdle when you know what the river might still have in store.

The first day Russ and I didn't observe a single hatch. There were no insects rising or fishing nibbling. There was only the flash of a few fish. Cutthroats frequently bite fish attractor patterns such as terrestrial's stimulators: grasshoppers, Turk tarantulas, Chernobyl ants, Wulff stoneflies, and mayflies.

When these aren't working, Russ will use a nymph submerged under the water. A strike indicator floating on the surface lets the angler know when a fish strikes. If this fails, he will use a streamer, a bright pink fly that is stripped through the water by the angler.

The second day, we put in at Fernie to float to the village of Morrissey. This section of the river, flowing through temperate rainforest surrounded by white and Engelmann spruce, old growth cedar, Douglas fir, aspen, and cottonwood, had more rapids than the previous day. Two golden eagles soared near their nest while a bald eagle flapped along the river. Riverbanks were blossoming with yellow daisies, blue lupine, and bright pink fireweed. We floated Elk, bear, Bighorn sheep, moose, elk, and deer inhabit the area.

Late in the afternoon, a rainstorm passed through, and as drops pounded us, we spied that magical long awaited sight of an insect hatch and trout rising to feed. We put our 5-weight 4x tippet rods into action releasing five beautiful cutthroats. They glistened with prominent orange slashes on the underside of their gill plates. It was a grand finale.

Fernie is not a city known for its glitter, a place where the trendy sport designer clothes, live in palatial homes, or dine in upscale restaurants. Its history is that of a coal-mining town, one surrounded by the grey limestone peaks of the Canadian Rockies Lizard range is the East Kootenay region of British Columbia.

Its architecture appears like that of a ski village with peaks surrounded by vertical slopes that attract powder buffs lusting for radical jumping and schussing. But summer visitors flock to Fernie to fish the Elk, a river that flows a distance of 100 miles from the Kootenay River. Anglers are hooked on the river's blue ribbon native cutthroat trout.

West Chilcotin Introduction

West Chilcotin, British Columbia is best known for its sport fishing. Many lakes are cold with clean water. They host freshwater shrimp, food that enables wild rainbow trout to grow strong and healthy.

The Turner Lake Chain is inhabited by Dolly Varden in addition to rainbow trout. Some lakes and streams offer coastal cutthroat trout. Ralph Edwards, who pioneered Lonesome Lake long before the Park was formed, stocked the region with trout fingerlings from the Atnarko River system.

The Upper Dean River is renowned for its fly fishing. Known for its rainbows, operators can fly anglers on the swampy headwaters of the River. Atnarko and Bella Coola Rivers are a place to fish for pink, Chinook, and coho salmon using flies, artificial wool, and spoons.

Many of the southern lakes are loaded with fish. Chilko Lake has rainbow trout up to six pounds. Chinook and sockeye salmon return to the Lake each year to spawn near the outlet. Salmon fry, in addition to abundant insect hatches, provides food for the trout.

While the Chilcotin offers remote lodges that are fly-in only, frequently the angler will have an entire lake or river to himself or herself.
(Source: West Chilcotin Tourism Association)

A Mary L. Peachin Adventure

Fly Fishing on the Upper Dean

Wading the Upper Dean River, located in remote north central British Columbia, a floatplane hop from Anahim Lake and Stewart's or Moosehead Lodges, we discovered the mother lode of wild, native trout fishing.

Thousands of resident and hybrid trout, some migrating from nearby Anahim Lake, populate the river. As for anglers, well, there are only a few. The fishery is a well-kept secret, one protected by limited angler fishing days.

The wilderness is populated by the First Nation's village of Anahim Lake and a lumber mill. Tweedsmuir Air, operated by Stewart's Lodge, provides a 20-minute flight to the water lily-lined "runway" on Abuntlet Lake.

At the Upper Dean headwaters is a cached 8-horse-powered flat-bottomed boat that powers anglers 3-4 miles to prime fishing holes, banks, and riffles. Anglers can wade a series of banks and holes until rapids make the river impassible.

Three of us enjoyed the best fishing days of our life throwing stimulators and seducers and both wet and dry flies using 4x tippets. On good days almost any colorful fly worked. The decision of which fly to use is sometimes determined on the decision to hook up on every cast or being more patient to enjoy the thrill of watching a fish rise on a dry.

While the Dean typically fishes well, the season opens June 15th and closes either when the river becomes too shallow or the weather turns too cold.

Added to its untapped fish population are great wading conditions. Currents flow gently over a sandy bottom, although there are spotty areas of boulders and weeds. In some places it's possible to wade in the middle of the Dean and fish either bank.

There was barely time to enjoy observing chattering bald-headed eagles, and flocks of golden eye and merganser ducks. The blue ribbon river fishes well because the steep elevation of the Chilcotin region makes it inaccessible to salmon, allowing trout to dominate the watershed.

Stewarts Lodge, www.stewartslodge.com

Langara's Moosehead Lodge

Moosehead Lodge, Langara Fishing Adventures fresh water operation, offers a unique fishing experience for avid fly anglers. The Lodge is also a retreat for small groups and families. Each summer Langara's offer a summer fly fishing camp for children ages of 11 and older.

Located in British Columbia's interior Chilcotin region, this rustic lakeside lodge is surrounded on all sides by rugged wilderness and is accessible only by floatplane.

The Chilcotin is known for its freshwater fly fishing. A trip to Moosehead Lodge provides access to numerous lakes and rivers throughout the region, including blue ribbon Blackwater and Upper Dean rivers.

British Columbia's diversity is evident in the high plateau country of West Chilcotin region and Moosehead Lodge on Moose Lake. Snow-capped mountains in the background frame a landscape of rivers and streams dissecting pine forests, alpine meadows, desert-like plateaus, towering waterfalls, and hundreds of square miles of remote terrain. Wildlife includes: grizzlies, deer, caribou, and moose. Numerous species of birds vary from pelicans and sea gull to ducks, Canada geese, loons, and blue grouse.

Moosehead Lodge accommodates 8-10 anglers in the same upscale style that anglers experience in their Haida Gwaii operation. Well-appointed lakeside cabins are complete with fireplaces, satellite television, and a fully stocked bar.

Moose Lake, located at an elevation of 3500 feet (1000 m) is five miles (8 km) long and half a mile (1 km) wide. Having no significant water inflow, Moose Lake is home to pure wild rainbow trout stock. They feed between May and October, and can be fished with wet or dry flies.

Wet flies are effective all season long, particularly following the spring thaw early in the season. A trout taking a wet fly can be so gentle that the only indication is a subtle line movement on the glassy water surface. A variety of dry flies can be fished throughout the season, particularly during the frequent insect hatches of mid and late summer.

All areas of Moose Lake can be fished, shoreline shallows to deep mid-lake waters, from the small islet in the east corner of the Lake to casting directly off the dock at the Lodge. Guests can navigate Moose Lake in float tubes, motor or pontoon boats.

Trophy Lake is a small lake south of Moose Lake. A half-day excursion, the lake is a 45-minute hike through surrounding forest. Fishing may be slower, but Trophy Lake regularly produces trout larger than those at Moose Lake. Anglers have the availability of a rowboat or they can carry in float tubes. Wet and dry flies, or spinners, are effective.

Floatplane excursions can be chartered to provide access throughout the region as well as unique sightseeing opportunities in this rugged landscape. Motor and pontoon boats, float tubes, and a canoe are also available for touring the lake. Non-fishing activities include hiking, horseshoeing, fly tying or casting lessons, or a soak in a wood-fired hot tub.

In the heart of the Chilcotin wilderness, Langara's dining at Moosehead Lodge sets a standard. All meals and alcohol are included in their fishing packages and quality is a common ingredient. The Lodge offers the finest and freshest ingredients to enable the head chef to prepare generous meals paired with wine. Dinners are served family-style in the dining cabin, while the lakeside patio is used for breakfast and lunch.

Anglers wanting to fly fish in emote and road-less wilderness will enjoy a trip to Moosehead Lodge with its easy access to excellent freshwater fishing.

(Source: Langara Fishing Adventures)

www.langara.com

A Mary L. Peachin Adventure

Stewart's Lodge On Nimpo Lake

Along the shoreline of Nimpo Lake, in the Chilcotin area of British Columbia, Beavers are tied to the piers of lakefront log cabins—not the furry animals, but the 1950s-era De Havilland aircraft. The 6-passenger single-engine floatplane can take off and land short, all while carrying a heavy load. Floatplanes like the Beaver, one of the most common means of travel in remote Canada, provide the perfect vehicle for a family fly fishing wilderness vacation.

Stewart's Lodge, built in the early '50s by Robert and Virginia Stewart, was originally a rustic tented fishing camp. Today, the lodge offers anglers a selection of eight nicely appointed cabins, each handcrafted of native lodgepole pine. The main lodge overlooks Nimpo Lake, backed by the snowcapped glacial peaks of Canada's coastal Cascade Range.

The closest village is located about 10 miles north of Nimpo. Anahim Lake, a small logging and farming community, has a 3,500-foot airstrip with daily air service from Vancouver provided by Pacific Coastal Airlines. 700 Chinook-speaking Ulkatcho Indians reside in the village and the surrounding communities of the Chilcotin Plateau—Carrier, Chilcotin, and Bella Coola.

Lodge owner Duncan Stewart checks the weather each morning; after consulting with visiting anglers, he decides their destination for the day. One of three pilots then loads the anglers (with their fishing gear and a bag lunch) into the lodge's Beaver. After 10-30 minutes of flying, the pilot delivers the anglers to one of many remote lakes or rivers for the day. This is "fly-in, fly-out" fishing.

Chief pilot Doug Clarke, a resident of nearby Williams Lake, has been piloting anglers for 20 years. Soon after our family group squeezed into his plane, we were treated to some sightseeing en route, most of it elements of Tweedsmuir Provincial Park. Our view included a spectacular view of the Monarch ice fields—majestic blue-ice glaciers whose jagged peaks trickled into jade-green glacial lakes. We also passed Huhlen Falls, a magnificent waterfall that pours into a gorge, as well as the Rainbow Mountains, a vertical collage of red, yellow, and black stone that belied a high concentration of copper and iron.

Early in the week, Doug dropped us at the Upper Dean River, one of the province's finest fisheries. The river is noted for daily catch-and release yields of 50-100 or more rainbow trout. Jumping from the Beaver's pontoons onto the shore, we then took a small-motorized boat upriver to one of the outpost cabins. On the river, fishing guide Paul Lowrie of Anahim River, BC pointed out pools and riffles filled with trout. Paul also led us through the swift currents and helped us wade around the slippery algae-covered boulders.

As we threw fly lines into the current, we were joined by bald eagles, which circled until they spotted trout, and then swooped down to grab the fish with their talons. A ruffled immature eagle stared down at us from one of the tall lodgepole pines. A golden-eye duck passed along the bank of the river, followed by a string of chicks.

As an alternative to river wading, we spent some time trolling the scenic lakes for brilliant speckled rainbow trout. Serious anglers might scoff at this method of fly fishing, but lake trolling offered a variety of surprises. One afternoon on Lake Eliquk, although the fish didn't discriminate between flies, red seemed to be the color of choice. Another time, the flash-a-bugger black/olive size six was the hot fly. In our group, the most consistent fly was the muddler.

Perhaps the most exciting thing about fishing on Lake Eliquk was watching a young bull moose, his antlers draped in velvet, take a swim, and then settle on the shoreline to warm in the sun. The glacier-covered mountains loomed behind the thick forest of black spruce and lodgepole pine, and the trout began to bite near the marshes. Late in the afternoon Doug Clarke guided the floatplane down to the lake and we reluctantly climbed aboard. We were back in Nimpo in 20 minutes, ready for dinner.

Hilda Reimer, the Stewart's Lodge chef, wore hiking boots and jeans; she seemed as comfortable outdoors as in the kitchen. At Stewart's, the fare is simple and hearty, but far from routine. Dinners featured fresh halibut, chicken, or steak tenderloin served with fresh vegetables and salads. We also enjoyed fresh desserts, homemade by a local pastry chef. Each morning, Hilda sent each of us out with a packed lunch, a thermos of coffee, and a sandwich. Breakfast was wonderful: our freshly caught trout, blueberry pancakes, bacon sausage, and hash browns.

One day we fished Lake Hotnarko, a 15-minute flight from the lodge. Because the day was windy, David, Suzie, and I shared a boat with a 3-horsepower engine—the engine's weight kept the boat from whirling in circles. While the floatplane pilot had assured us that such engines "never run out of gas," the impossible came to pass; we relied on a fortunate tailwind and some frantic paddling to return to the dock. Taking a break after adding the fuel, Suzie spotted a grouse with her chicks, a bald eagle, and several loons.

After a few days of fishing, Suzie had to return to her job in

Portland. David and I were eager to camp out in one of Stewart's "outpost cabins," half a dozen cozy wilderness structures nestled along the shorelines and beaches of remote lakes and rivers. The cabins come stocked with food, linens, and wood for the campfire or wood-burning stove.

We chose what the brochure touted as "the perfect honeymoon cabin", a small structure built on a sandy beach in a private cove on Davidson Lake, surrounded by the snow-capped peaks of Mt. Davidson; the mountain's snowmelt trickles into springs that feed the lake. Outside the cabin, two wooden beach chairs arranged next to a tree-stump table offered wonderful views of the mountains. A small motorized boat was tied to the pier; a canoe rested against the cabin wall.

In each of the outpost cabins, cooking can be done on the outdoor campfire or in the cabin's wood-burning or propane stoves. The lake provides drinking water; the cupboard is filled with canned provisions and supplemented by the lodge's provisions of eggs, milk, potatoes, and T-bone steaks. Lunch, however, was a different story. Faced with a meal of peanut butter or tuna, I amended my "catch-and-release" philosophy and headed out to hook some lunch. Freshly cooked trout straight from the lake and grilled on the campfire is scrumptious.

Stewart's practices "catch and release" and encourages anglers to release the trout in the water with not even taking the opportunity for a photograph.

At bedtime, we stoked the fire and patrolled the cabin for large, slow-flying British Columbia mosquitoes. Snuggled under thick quilts, we fell asleep listening to the crackling of the fire and the distinctive call of the loon.

The next day, offered the opportunity by Duncan Stewart to stream fish for cutthroat trout, we took a scenic flight over Huhlen Falls before landing at the campsite of Turner Lake. After a mile of hiking, we reached an excellent fishing spot where Cutthroat Lake feeds into the Huhlen stream. Three of us caught and released more than 30 of this smaller species of trout.

In "rust-colored" lakes like Gatcho, there is a better opportunity to catch trout weighing more than two pounds. We learned that this color comes from an algae bloom, one that supports freshwater shrimp, which feed larger trout. This is especially true in the Blackwater watershed of the Chilcotin area.

While we were casting our fly lines, several canoes paddled downstream; we had noticed wooden racks along the trail, which, Duncan explained, are used to rest the canoes between portages. After fishing our way upstream, we made it back to the Turner Lake campground, where we waited for our floatplane. There we talked with three canoers, who told us about the three to five day canoe route through Tweedsmuir Provincial Park.

It turns out that the Turner Lake chain also offers camping at Junker, Widgeon, and Kidney Lakes; most sites allow superb views of Talchako Mountain and Mt. Ratcliff. The campgrounds are meticulous; tent plots are covered with sand to create level ground for sleeping. Each site has a grill and picnic table.

Here, canoe trips are launched much like fly-in, fly-out fishing: canoes are tied to the airplane pontoons and flown into the area. Years ago, a ranger named Ralph Edwards helped to create the route in Tweedsmuir Park by installing piers and portage signs between the lakes.

Flying out to Squiness Lake, also in the park, we sighted a black bear and a herd of mountain goats atop the peaks of the Rainbow Mountains. The lake fishing was slow at first, but we caught and released big trout using flies of leeches and others including black and brown muddlers, a seducer, a Madam X, and a Royal Wulff. Along the shoreline we watched a Merganser duck protect her chicks by fighting off a marauding mink.

All winter, our family has reflected on the beauty of this majestic, isolated region of British Columbia. In one week, we released more trout than we have seen in a lifetime.
www.stewartslodge.com

Vancouver Island

Introduction

Vancouver Island, with the exception of New Zealand, is the largest Pacific island. Victoria, the capital city of British Columbia, is located on the southeast coast. The city of Vancouver is located on the North American mainland.

In the late 18th century, the island was explored by British and Spanish expeditions arrived. The Island is named after George Vancouver, the British Royal Navy officer who explored the Pacific Northwest coast of North America between 1791 and 1794. The island is 290 miles long (460 k), 50 miles wide (80 k), and covers 12,407 square miles (32,134 sq.km.)

Anglers are more inclined to stay at resorts, lodges, or inns near Kyuquot, Nootka Sound, Gold River, Tofino, Ucluelet, Port Alberni, Sooke, Victoria, Nanaimo, and Campbell River to fish with private guides. The majority of dedicated fishing operations are located near the northwest coast.

Covering 12,355 square miles (32,000 sq.km), Vancouver Island, is the largest of North America's Pacific Ocean islands. One of approximately 6,000 islands in British Columbia, it covers 285 miles (460 km) in length and is 62 miles (100 km) wide. The mountainous spine covers its length reaches into long mountain fjords along the west coast. Mt. Golden Hinde, in Strathcona Provincial Park, at 7,218 feet (2,200 m) is the tallest point on Vancouver Island.

Surrounded by ocean, Vancouver Island has an extensive network of rivers, lakes and streams including Della Falls, one of Canada's highest waterfalls. The Island is separated from British Columbia's mainland by the Strait of Georgia and from Washington State by the Strait of Juan de Fuca. The west coast of Vancouver Island is largely unpopulated.

(Courtesy of Hello BC)

Vancouver Island, located in southwestern British Columbia, is separated from the mainland by Johnstone Strait and Queen Charlotte Strait on the north and northeast, and by the Strait of Georgia on the southeast. The southwestern Strait of Juan de Fuca separates Vancouver Island from Washington State in the United States. The Straits of Georgia, Juan de Fuca, and Puget Sound are considered part of the Salish Sea. The Pacific Ocean runs along the west side of Vancouver Island, to its north is Queen Charlotte Sound.

The Alberni Inlet cuts more than halfway through the island ending at the community of Port Alberni. Victoria's Saanich Inlet is one of the few fjord inlets on Vancouver Island's east coast.

Tourism Vancouver Island, www.tourismvi.ca
Tourism Victoria, www.tourismvictoria.com
Tourism Tofino, www.tourismtofino.com
Tourism Nanaimo, www.tourismnanaimo.com

Critter Cove

Located in the heart of Nootka Sound, the marina is 30 miles (18 km) by water from the village of Gold River. Between June and October, salmon return to the Conuma River and several other rivers in Nootka. The calm waters of the Sound are an attraction for those who wish not to venture into open water.

Experienced self-contained anglers can find accommodations like marine gas, tackle store, bait, ice, as well as a restaurant. Accommodations range from floating bunkhouse cabins to self-contained beach cottages or simply mooring. www.crittercove.com

Homefray Lodge

Homfray Lodge in isolated Desolation Sound's Homfray Channel, accessible only by boat or floatplane, is near Foster Point. Surrounded by remote and pristine water, the Lodge is located 100 miles north of Vancouver. Family-owned and operated by brothers David, Matthew, and Scott Macey, this destination and lodge is a good choice for experienced anglers and cruisers who are primarily looking for moorage.

The lodge offers an assortment of accommodation options including spacious and open cabins, with kitchenettes, that sleep six, as well as smaller rooms for two. A communal cookhouse has modern amenities to create a great meal. There are four tent sites with access to common bathrooms and the cookhouse. Ridge Row contains five suites, which can sleep three anglers with a queen and single bed, plus a private bath and shower. The Great Room in the main Lodge can be booked for larger groups or events.

Family meals or quick snacks can be made in the cookhouse. Anglers are expected to bring their own food, do their own cooking, and clean up.

Homefray Lodge offers a limited amount of guided fishing for up to three anglers. There are bottom fish in Homfray Channel or Chinook around nearby Toba Inlet. More serious anglers can fish in Bute Inlet, Stewart Island, or Big Bay for all species of salmon and bottom fish.

(Source: Homefray Lodge)

www.homfraylodge.com

Dolphins Resort

A well-kept secret on Vancouver Island is Dolphins Resort. Located 10 minutes north of downtown Campbell River, this enchanting destination offers Pan-abode cabins. Constructed of Western red cedar, these cabins, surrounded by flower gardens and fir trees, have a great view of Discovery Passage. Uniquely furnished with antiques and wood burning fireplaces, they offer an ambiance of warmth and old-fashioned charm.

Offering more than saltwater, fly fishing, and heli-fishing, anglers can top their day soaking in a steamy hot tub outside their door as they plan the next day's adventure.

The Anglers Dining Room at Dolphins resort features gourmet cuisine served in an oceanfront setting. Open to the public, Anglers features an Italian-inspired seafood menu reflecting the seasonal bounty of Campbell River and Vancouver Island.

Fishing packages include an ocean front or garden view cabins with an individual outdoor hot tub, daily gourmet dinner, continental or full breakfast depending on time of fishing departure, boxed lunch including soft drinks, bottled water or juice, and guided saltwater salmon fishing with all gear and tackle in a covered cabin cruiser with onboard head.

There are "Beginner's Luck" packages to those offering 16 or even 24 hours of fishing. Dolphins Resort can be much more than fishing. Activities include hiking, kayaking, whale watching, snorkeling with salmon, bear viewing, bird watching, bicycling, or a helicopter tour.

Flight services from either Seattle or Vancouver by either float plane or multiple scheduled airlines.

(Source: Dolphins Resort)
www.dolphinsresort.com

Murphy's Kyuquot Sound Lodge

Murphy's Sportfishing operates this 33-angler lodge adjacent to the small village of Kyuquot. Siblings David and Marilyn Murphy, both Vancouver Island iconic lifelong avid anglers, have the expertise to know exactly what anglers need and expect on a fishing trip. Providing excellent guides and top notch equipment, plentiful salmon, halibut, their fishing grounds are minutes away. They claim, "We're perched on the edge of the 'Super Salmon Highway' with our peak season between June and mid-September".

In addition to its fishing, wildlife including the seldom-viewed sea otter, eagles, and whales are plentiful. For several weeks at the end of August, Dave Murphy offer albacore fishing located 15 to 25 miles offshore.

Late summer warmer water currents flow towards Kyuquot, attracting pelagics to follow their food source as currents move further north and closer to the British Columbia shore.

Murphy's treat caught fish with care. All fish are bled immediately then stored in the vessels cool "fish hold." Anglers determine and inform the dock whether they would like the fish left whole or fileted. Each fish is individually tagged with your personal trip ID #, bagged, and placed in cold storage for the duration of the trip. The first day's catch will be frozen, the balance of your catch chilled hard, and then suitable for travel or further processing.

The Lodge offers comfortable accommodations. All meals are provided during the angler's stay with a hearty breakfast, boxed lunch, and delicious dinner. Their boats are fully equipped Transport Canada approved vessels.

They boast professional, experienced personable guides. All equipment and rain gear is supplied with the exception of boots.

There are numerous options for getting to Kyuquot Sound Lodge. There is a 3-hour shuttle from Fair Harbour on active gravel logging road, a floatplane from Vancouver, Victoria, or Campbell River. BC Ferries and commercial flights are available between Vancouver and Campbell River.

Murphy's have been operating two fishing accommodations in Kyuquot for more than 20 years. In 2016, the *MV Daleanne One* will be retired and their land-based lodge expanded to accommodate those anglers.

www.murphysportfishing.com

A Mary L. Peachin Adventure

Captain Marilyn Murphy's salmon fishing briefing begins on the stern of the MV Daleanne One. As she speaks, a black bear lumbers along a nearby the beach. "Kyuquot," she explains, ignoring the animal, "translates to land of many winds." Unfazed by the distraction, she outlines British Columbia's salmon and halibut regulations to a dozen hard-core anglers. "Don't worry, that's just Boo," the 4-year-old resident bear, she says. "During low tide, he scavenges the beach for shells and other inter-tidal critters."

It's just another fishing day anchored behind Surprise Island, where the Daleanne floats in the lee of a cove about a 5-minute boat ride from the First Nations village of Kyuquot. For the next three nights, the 83-foot, 97,000-ton ship housing 10 bunks, four shared baths, and two showers will be home to salmon anglers, most of whom are return visitors, Daleanne devotees. The Murphy's welcome old friends with enthusiastic laughs and hugs.

The journey to Kyuquot is an interesting one. After transferring from Seattle or Vancouver, anglers can fly or ferry to Campbell River, a village on the east coast of Vancouver Island. The adventure begins on the island highway heading toward Woss, a 2-lane road that winds through old-growth rainforest. There are beautiful views of emerald-green lakes, many framed by the Vancouver Island range's snowcapped peaks. Black bear, cougar, and Roosevelt elk inhabit the area. The paved road ends a few miles with a final hour-drive on maintained logging roads via Zeballos to Fair Harbour. At the end of the road, anglers are greeted by Murphy's fleet of boats that shuttle them a scenic 45-minute boat ride to their accommodation.

Eager to meet their guides, anglers hurriedly jump into 24- to 26-foot boats and head for some deep-water, down rigging, open-ocean salmon fishing.

Captain Marilyn Murphy has fished since childhood. She's been a guide for the family-operated Murphy Sportfishing almost half of her life, and can tie knots, set out lines, find fish, and out fish almost anyone. She was taught by "one of the best," her father Gordon—who, in his 70's, was still guiding in Barkley Sound near Port Alberni.

In recent years, Marilyn spends her time managing the larger lodge. She does have her own 24-foot Grady White boat tied to the dock so when the bite is on, she is out there for the catch.

25-knot winds are the norm, and Marilyn will fish up to 10-foot seas with northwesterly winds up to 40 knots. Anglers with queasy stomachs can find calmer waters near the shore in the lee of the Barrier Islands, a group of lava rock formations that provides some protection from the elements.

When her introduction is complete—an excellent meal consumed—we head out to troll using downriggers, to depths of 120 feet for Chinook or king salmon. Scanning the water, Marilyn searches for salmon as she steers the boat. She's looking for birds, particularly murrelets, a species that dives to 120 feet. "These birds will sit on top of the same feed where Chinook are feeding. She's also looking for surface bait, or fish appearing on her fish finder. She knows the topography of the reefs and ridges and where salmon tend to feed. This area produces good fishing for salmon that have not yet headed to their spawning rivers, and anglers almost always catch their daily limits.

Salmon feed on pilchards, needlefish, anchovies, and squid, so Marilyn baits a squid-like "hoochie" with a bright colored flasher. A 20-pound-ish Chinook immediately took the bait. We start trolling in late afternoon; by the time we head for the ship four hours later, Kyuquot is shrouded in fog. Marilyn has to rely on the boat's radar to navigate some shallow channels avoiding treacherous rocks.

Our second day, we opt for some light-tackle coho fishing. While hatchery-bred coho, their back fin clipped, can be kept, Marilyn gently releases the wild ones. This type of fishing produces a lot better results, plus using lighter tackle is a lot more fun.

Our final morning, we decide to fish behind the lee of Spring and Thornton Island. We begin by trolling for salmon with 9-weight fly rods, trailing flashers, and fly streamers called "bucktails." I find salmon striking a fly more exciting than the bent rod experienced in deep-water fishing. I take a break and look around, enjoying the shore's black-lava rocks covered with gulls and cormorants, spruce trees capping each small island, and bull kelp gleaming in the sunshine.

"I love the smell of low tide," Marilyn tells me as she inhales a whiff of kelp, eelgrass, barnacles, and starfish. She takes another breath and smiles. "We'll be doing some gardening today," she laughs, referring to de-weeding our flies.

Marilyn loves her life and loves fishing. Along with her husband, brother, and 12 other guides, she'll work nonstop from June to August before heading the boat back to Point Alberni. It's a long season, but by fall, she'll be ready for eight weeks of managing their fall river fishery program followed by the winter steelhead season at their Stamp River Lodge.

Sounds exhausting, right? Ah, but in November, she and her husband will take a month of vacation. They'll go fishing somewhere warm and you will find her fly fishing while wading the flats somewhere in the tropics.

Nootka Island Lodge

One of Vancouver Island's original fishing lodges, Nootka Island Lodge, located 25 miles west of Gold River, is surrounded by a forest

of cedars, spruce and fir along the tranquil waters of Nootka Sound.

The lodge, which offers both single- and double-occupancy, has a capacity for 20 guests. Family-style dining, served by their attentive staff includes appetizers and beverages. BYOB cocktails are welcomed. The Cyr's serve fish nightly as well as rib eye steak, Danish Baby Back Ribs, chicken, roast beef with Yorkshire pudding, or maybe a pork loin roast.

The Cyr family, four generations of them, has owned and operated the lodge for more than three decades. Terry and Bette-Anne Cyr purchased the old town site of Nootka, where the cannery was located, in 1982. They built and opened the Lodge in 1983. Their children, Tim and Sandy, who worked at the Lodge since its opening, purchased the Lodge from their parents in the late 1990s.

All of the Cyr family belongs to the Nootka Island Lodge including son Matt and his wife Kym, and grandchildren Carter and Natalie. Matt and Kym's daughter Katie Mangles and her husband Ash, grandchildren Austyn, Mason, and newborn Natalie are also considered part of the team. The Cyr's are a family dedicated to roviding you the experience of a lifetime - that is the essence of Nootka Island Lodge.

The lodge's fishing targets Chinook and Coho, as well as bottom fishing for halibut, lingcod, and Yellow Eye rockfish. Included in their 8-hour guided fishing day in 16- to 24-foot boats with Yamaha engines, they supply all fishing gear including rain suits and boots. Nootka Island Lodge fillet, provide ice packs, or vacuum seal the angler's catch.

Wildlife is plentiful on the commute to the fishing grounds and includes whales, bald eagles, otters, and a variety of sea birds.

Nootka Sound Lodge was originally purchased from Nootka Packing Company in 1917 by WR Lord, Sr. It served as a salmon saltery in Friendly Cove, with a cannery and reduction plant added later. It is believed that the operation closed in the 1960s.

(Source: Nootka Island Lodge)

www.nootkaislandlodge.com

WESTERN FISHERIES   *June, 1936*

B. C. FISHERY

NOOTKA PACKING AND FISHING COMPANY, OPERATING THE NOOTKA PACKING CO. LTD.

THE Langara plant in Mascott Inlet, Q.C.I., is managed by Alec Furguson; the Nootka plant on the west coast of Vancouver Island by D. W. Wilson; the Tow Hil plant, and the home of the famous Snow Cap Minced Razor Clams, will not operate this season.

In 1917, W. R. Lord, Senior, started a saltery at the present Nootka location. He interested the Everett Packing Co. in the idea of building a salmon cannery at this point, from which sprang the Nootka Packing Co. Ltd. In 1925 the reduction of fish meal and oil was inaugurated and today this company produces about 75% of the total fish meal and oil output of British Columbia. In 1934 the projects were carried on by the operating Nootka Packing and Fishing Co. Ltd., which carries on the finest canning plant on the B. C. Pacific coast, as well as the other units mentioned.

The Langara Fishing and Packing Co., started by the late Mr. Simpson, who continued as manager for many years, was acquired by the Nootka Packing Co.

The late J. J. Petrich came to Nootka in 1926, a year after the reduction plant was installed, and continued as general manager and president of the company until his death in 1935. The present officers are President L. L. Crosby and General Manager and Secretary-Treasurer S. M. Rosenberg.

Mr. A. C. Goble, the head office accountant, has been identified with the fishing industry for many years. His career takes us back to the days when Tom Lake was manager of the Carlyle Cannery on the Skeena River, with Curtis Butterfield as

to be compared with bringing coals to Newcastle, but the epicurean demands, through the caterer, can always be met by the Vancouver Shell Fish Co. They have shad roe from the Columbia River, or turtles for turtle soup from the West Indies. Truly, here is one firm that handles everything that swims.

NELSON BROTHERS FISHERIES LIMITED

THE western fishing industry has watched with a good deal of interest the quiet yet progressive development of this concern. The partnership established between R. Nelson and N. Nelson in 1920 has evolved to fishery operation of a wide character. Then the Nelson Brothers Fisheries Limited was incorporated in 1929. Operations included the reduction of pilchard, herring and the by-products therefrom, in addition to pretentious operations in dry salt herring and dry salt salmon production. They entered the canning field in 1933, with the Canadian Packing Company canning herring, pilchard and all of the salmon species.

A broad background of experience enters into the operations when we introduce Marsh English in charge of the St. Mungo cannery on the Fraser River, and another veteran, shall we say, of the younger school, D. T. Lutz, manager of the Ceepeecee plant on the west coast of Vancouver Island.

OCEAN FISHERIES LIMITED

THE Royal Fish Co. was bought out in 1924 by Mr. H. R. Nobouka, who had been connected with this concern for five years, and in this venture he was joined by his present partner, Mr. G. Isogai. They began to expand production and trading

(1936 article courtesy of Canfisco)

Rugged Point Lodge

Kyuquot Sound, on Vancouver Island's northwest coast, is home to the small, protected village of Walter's Cove. Built in 2011, Rugged Point Lodge, overlooking the Sound, is a charming twelve guest fishing lodge. Its six guest ensuite rooms have the added comfort of a large salon with dining area, and a lounge. Warmed by a wooden stove, its seating area overlooks an ocean view deck.

Saltwater fishing season begins in May and ends the first week in September. Salmon fishing in the spring and summer is excellent when salmon migrating south from the Columbia River system feed in surrounding waters. Halibut fishing is excellent throughout the season.

Albacore tuna fishing begins approximately the third week of August lasting until late in September. Rugged Point Lodge is twenty-seven miles to South Brooks Buoy, a place where albacore congregate. This Environment Canada weather station provides wave and swell height, wind speed and sea surface temperature. It also attracts fish.

The reel screams when an albacore descends at fifty miles per hour. Following the first hookup they troll for a minute to hook more fish. The boat is then put into neutral creating a "glide." Anglers without a hookup now cast a bait or vertical jig while others are playing the fish. There are times when a school of tuna will remain around the boat eliminating the need to troll. Albacore fishing can be an exciting happening.

Tuna fishing is weather dependent. Calm seas and good water currents are required. In the five years since Rugged Point Lodge began targeting these fish they have enjoyed a 90% success rate. Using satellite imagery, long range forecasts, and years of local experience, they place their boats in the water at the right time and in the right spot. Their guides are experienced commercial and sport tuna fisherman who love fishing albacore.

Their boats are geared with six trolling rods and two casting rods. When fishing for albacore they generally fish a four to six rod spread. Once they get "take downs" or "fish on" the excitement of seeing tuna schools cruising like dolphins across the ocean towards the fishing gear is heart-stopping. Other times the tuna daisy chain, jump, chase the trolling spread or Pacific saury bait fish. When tuna hit the bait, it feels like the stern of the boat explodes with action.

In September, Rugged Point Lodge guides put on their waders to head up one of the six surrounding rivers for some fall fly fishing. They offer guided walk-and-wade and raft or inflatable jet boat trips. Accompanied by boats for transportation, the rivers are easily waded with casts varying between forty to sixty feet.

The fish are bright chrome and later in the season there is a blend of bright fish and colored fish. They catch coho and chum into early November, some still have sea lice attached, an indication that they have recently migrated from salt water. Sharing the rivers with black bear and Roosevelt elk, and paw prints of cougar and wolf is a true wilderness adventure.

Kyuquot is accessible by air or water. Located south of Brooks Peninsula and north of Nootka Island, travel options include driving to Fair Harbour, a three and a half hour drive north west of Campbell River. There is also the option of taking a float plane.
(Source Rugged Point Lodge)
www.ruggedpointlodge.com

The Lodge at Gold River

The Lodge at Gold River defines "the luxury of roughing it." They offer guided fishing on some of west coast Vancouver Island's wild steelhead and trout rivers as well as salmon fishing in the renowned waters of Nootka Sound. The Lodge offers a variety of angling experiences suitable to the anglers' level of experience. Boats, helicopters, and floatplanes are used for guiding to enable them to offer access to watersheds accessible only by air. Paired with an experienced local guide staff, the Lodge at Gold River can create a remote angling adventure. They also offer unique and exciting non-fishing activities.

The Lodge's British Columbian spruce and pine log building is located on 1,200 feet. Its main lodge is impressive in a comfortable setting. Following a day filled with adventure, anglers can relax on the outdoor patio to enjoy a fine meal centered by an outdoor fireplace.

Designed to accommodate food and beverage service, the main lounge is the central gathering area for guests. It features an entertainment and bar area with a 50-inch large screen television, card tables, shuffleboard table, and areas to simply sit and relax. Locally carved west coast First Nations masks complement the dining room. Their Executive Chef specializes in serving West Coast cuisine including fresh seafood and locally raised Vancouver Island venison.

Additionally, The Lodge features several cabins with three separate guestrooms. Each bedroom has two queen size beds, a wood burning fireplace, a furnished sitting area, and granite-appointed bathroom suites.

These spacious 540 square feet rooms offer picturesque river and mountain views with amenities including hair dryers, individual climate controls, telephone, high-speed wireless Internet access, CD player, remote-controlled cable television, air-conditioning, and a comfortable seating area with opening windows.

During summer, fishing shifts from winter steelhead to lake and stream fishing for trout. Dry fly fishing can be excellent even when anglers remain close to The Lodge. Another option includes stalking riverbanks for summer run steelhead.

Summer salmon fishing takes places in Nootka Sound in cruiser-style boats roomy enough for three or four anglers. Fall's focus is centered on returning salmon as they stage in rivers to complete their spawning journey.

The Lodge is located along Highway 28 on the west coast of Vancouver Island east of Campbell River. Staff greets anglers at Campbell River airport for arriving Central Mountain Air, Pacific Coastal, or Kenmore Air daily flights from Vancouver and Seattle.

For those traveling Vancouver by car, B.C. Ferries provides transportation. From Campbell River, The Lodge is about an hour by car through Strathcona Park, the largest provincial park on the Island.

(Source: The Lodge at Gold River)
www.thelodgeatgoldriver.ca

A Mary L. Peachin Adventure

Tofino: the King of Tides

Life in the Vancouver Island village of Tofino revolves around the tide. Folks begin their day by looking at the tidal charts. The 14-foot differential between high and low Pacific tides affects not just beach lovers but anglers, kayakers, scuba divers, surfers, and whale watchers. Even the local animals are affected; black bears and bald eagles schedule their feeding habits to scavenge the beach at low tide.

Tofino sits on a promontory at the far west end of Vancouver Island, a place where 2-lane Highway 4 ends at the coastline.

Historically a fishing port, this picturesque village, because of its isolation and the rugged beauty of its volcanic coastline, has in recent years become a tourist destination.

There's also the attraction of a wide variety of water sports. Near the Clayoquot Sound, adventure companies lure vacationers on salmon fishing trips, kayaking, and whale watching. Bright red "survival" suits hang on store doorframes. Shops may sell new kites or rent old mountain bikes.

The requisite quaint shops cater to visitors, while locals hangs out at food cart Tacofino or the bakery, which offers views of the harbor. Kayakers launch into the sound near the floatplane dock, while those going whale-watching meet under one or another red suit. Choices also include a trip to Hot Springs Cove, bear watching, or exploring a native village.

"The Wick", as locals call it, offers ocean views from every room, and guests drift into slumber to the sound of crashing waves, or watch the majestic sea from the Wick's Pointe Restaurant, cantilevered out over craggy volcanic rocks. This experience is the pride of general manager Charles McDiarmid, who's managed to sell visitors on coming to Tofino during winter months to watch violent winter storms raise the 20-foot waves that spray the floor-to-ceiling glass windows of the restaurant. To enhance the diner's experience, the sound of crashing waves is piped into the restaurant, along with a selection of classical music.

Outside of Tofino, the options for travelers are many. Nine

miles by boat from Tofino, but seemingly far from civilization, is Clayoquot Wilderness Resort. The luxurious safari-type camp is located near the Bedwell River.

Another option is the 7-mile (11 km) Ahousaht Wild Side Heritage Trail. Hikers are transported by boat from Tofino Harbour to Flores Island's Cow Bay. The trail opened in 1996 and features a mile of cedar-plank boardwalk through the boggier parts of the forest. Its eight miles of ups and downs, turns and twists through dense rainforest offer intervals of shell-strewn white sand beaches. A beautiful, challenging hike, the trail is marked by the myth and history of the Ahousaht people. At points along the route, signposts are accompanied by a series of placards sharing the myth and history of the Ahousaht First American Nation.

More beautiful views are available near Ucluelet, about 25 miles south of Tofino. The groomed Wild Pacific Trail winds along a rugged coastline revealing stunning Pacific views at every turn. Hikers can stop for lunch or a view at strategically placed cedar benches overlooking Pacific Ocean bays and coves.

Salmon draws anglers to the area. Serious fishermen time their fishing around the slack hours of the tide's flood and ebb, when the waters bring in the smaller sea life on which the fish feed.

A pod of orca or killer whales compete for the same feed, rolling, breaching, and "sky hopping" in circles, to the delight of whale watchers. Resident gray and occasional humpbacks can also be sighted.

Pacific Rim National Park Reserve ends a few miles outside of Tofino. It was established in 1970 as Canada's first Pacific coast national park. Campsites are available in the Park. Long Beach is a popular place for surfing, particularly during winter's higher surf.

Back at the beach, folks can dig for clams or search for oysters and sea urchins in tidal pools left by the outgoing waves. Kids hop from pool to pool, looking for brightly colored starfish and anemones.

From active sports to an appreciation of lovingly farmed mollusks with garlic butter, Tofino has a lot to offer the traveler. As Courtney Caton, son of former Clayoquot Wilderness Lodge manager John Caton, explains, the variety of life here is intimately tied to the tides: "The water level is never the same so you are always seeing something new and different."

Tofino

The west coast Vancouver Island village of Tofino, located on Esowista Peninsula, is at the terminus of Highway four. Wedged between the southern edge of Clayoquot Sound and the Pacific Ocean. Considered a popular summer tourist destination, Tofino's population swells attracting anglers, surfers, nature lovers, campers, and whale watchers. Close to Tofino is Long Beach, also a scenic and popular year-round destination adjacent to Pacific Rim National Park Reserve.

There is every type of accommodation available in Tofino, but the history of the village and its growth as a tourist attraction can be attributed to the McDiarmid family.

January of 1955 marks the beginning of The Wickaninnish Inn history. Dr. Howard McDiarmid moved to Tofino to assume responsibility for Tofino General Hospital. Over the years, recognizing the area's unique nature, he was instrumental in the 1971 creation of the Pacific Rim National Park Reserve.

The establishment of the national park would eventually result in the conversion of the original Wickaninnish Inn to today's Marine Interpretive Centre. The Inn's closure sparked Howard's vision to recreate that rustic elegance into a modern hotel.

Inspired by their parents' foresight, the McDiarmid family joined with a group of long-time Tofino residents to make the Doctor's vision a reality. In August of 1996, a new Wickaninnish Inn opened housing The Pointe Restaurant. The natural appeal of Tofino as a destination and the quality experience provided by the Inn brought a steady growth of Canadian and international visitors.

In 2001, the McDiarmid's purchased full ownership, making the Inn a family-owned business. To fulfill long-term plans and meet growing demand, the Inn added an "On-the-Beach" building in July 2003.

The McDiarmid's vision of a hotel on Tofino's Chesterman Beach began with a desire to reflect the essence of Tofino as a rugged, wild, and untamed destination in combination with the ultimate in modern creature comforts – all without making a huge impact on the environment. Architecturally, the Inn has succeeded in defining an archetypal North West Coast style, utilizing the natural elements of cedar, fir, driftwood, and stone, together with expansive windows inviting the awe-inspiring ocean vistas. The Inn truly embodies its commitment to Rustic Elegance on Nature's Edge.

(Courtesy of Wickaninnish Inn)

www.wickinn.com

Fishing Charter Operators

Cameron Sport Fishing, cameronsportfishing.com

Hymax Charters, www.hymaxcharters.com

Ocean Outfitters, www.oceanoutfitters.com

Wardo West, www.wardowest.com

Tofino 1st Class Fishing, www.tofino1stclassfishing.com

Tofino Fish Guides, www.tofinofishguides.com

Victoria

The city was established in 1843 as a fort for the Hudson's Bay Company. Victoria's British ancestry is apparent in its double-decker buses, horse-drawn carriages, formal gardens, and tearooms. It is surrounded by ocean on three sides. Cliffs, spits, and lagoons, formed by glacial action, make up portions of the shoreline on the northern and western coastlines.

In other locations, the shoreline consists of beaches of pebble and sand, punctuated with coves. Victoria is a fishing hotspot that offers anglers easy access to the salmon-rich waters of the Pacific Ocean as well as the sheltered waterways of Georgia Strait and the Gulf Islands. Summer months are the time to fish salmon and halibut-filled waters off Vancouver Island's west coast. Victoria and its surrounding communities of Sidney, Sooke and Port Renfrew offer anglers of all skill levels an impressive choice of fishing opportunities. (Courtesy of Tourism Victoria)

Sooke Harbour House

An hour west of Victoria, the village of Sooke, was originally inhabited by the Coast Salish T'sou-ke Indians, a First Nation's band dependent on the area's berries, birds, clams and fish. In 1849, European settlers followed by the 1864 Leech River gold rush created a population boom. Today, the area is best known for Sooke Harbour House. The resort, overlooking the Salish Sea's Strait of Juan de Fuca is noted for its twenty-eight individually designed rooms, all recently refurnished.

Sooke Harbour House Resort Hotel, www.sookeharbourhouse.com
Sooke Salmon Charters, www.fishingbc1.com
Sooke Harbour Marina, www.sookeharbourmarina.ca
Sooke Fishing Adventures, www.fishingsooke.ca
Sooke Charter Fishing, www.goincoastalfishing.com

Lower Mainland

Richmond, BC's Gateway City to Sport Fishing

Vancouver International Airport, located in coastal Richmond, is British Columbia's 4th largest city. Packed with diversity, its Asian population (65 %) is the highest in Canada. Located on Lulu Island at the mouth of the Fraser River, Richmond includes the adjacent Sea Island along with a few uninhabited smaller islets. The Strait of Georgia lines its western border.

For years, Vancouver has been voted one of the top cities in the world to visit. Its beautiful mountain and ocean setting, cultural diversity, fine cuisine, luxury hotels, wonderful parks, and extensive attractions encourage anglers to take the time to explore Richmond, as well as Vancouver, and other areas of British Columbia rather than simply passing through its airport.

(Source: Tourism Richmond)
www.tourismrichmond.com

Angler-Friendly Hotels

Fairmont Airport Hotel: www.fairmont.com/vancouver-airport-richmond

River Rock Casino: www.riverrock.com/promotion/fishing/

Pacific Gateway Hotel: www.pacificgatewayhotel.com/hotel/fishing.htm

Four Points Sheraton Vancouver Airport, www.fourpointsvancouverairport.com

OPUS Hotel Versante will be located in the Mo Yeung's International Trade Centre development (opening Fall, 2017)

Things to Do

Historic Fishing Village of Steveston

Steveston is a British fishing village with Asian roots. Located where the Fraser River and Pacific Ocean converge, Steveston was established in the early 1800's during the fishing cannery boom. At the turn of the century, with 15 canneries, it boasted the largest fishing facility in the British Commonwealth. Steveston is a destination for West Coast shopping, dining, and exploring.

Fisherman's Wharf is a place to watch locals barter for the catch of the day when fishing boat arrive loaded with fresh salmon, crab, halibut. and shrimp. The waterfront village is known for its British-style fish and chips. There are whale-watching adventures or nature or historic tours with professional naturalists to view orca whales, porpoises, sea lions, bald eagles, and other wildlife.

Golden Village

Richmond's bustling commercial district is in the heart of the city. It's three Asian shopping malls offering the latest designer fashions from Hong Kong, Tokyo, and Taipei. "Wai Sek Kai" or "Food Street" on Alexandra Road hosts more than 200 authentic Asian restaurants packed into three short city blocks.

The diversity of Asian food cuisines includes Cantonese, Szechuan,

Shanghainese, Northern Chinese, Thai, Vietnamese, Korean, and Malaysian. Many of these eateries are tucked away in small strip malls in the area between Sea Island Way to the north, Garden City Road to the east, Alderbridge Way to the south, and No. 3 Road to the west.

International Buddhist Temple

The International Buddhist Society Kuan Yin Temple is considered the most magnificent and authentic temple of traditional Chinese architecture in North America. Golden porcelain tiles that glitter on its rooftop and intricacies with superb workmanship blending traditional Chinese art and culture makes this Buddhist temple similar to Beijing's Forbidden City.

There is a peaceful courtyard to view bonsai plants and a ceramic mural of Kuan-Yin-Bodhisattva. The artistic interior houses artifacts of Chinese workmanship in sculpture, painting, carpentry and embroidery. The Temple is located on 12 acres and serves one of the largest congregations of Buddhists in British Columbia. www.buddhisttemple.ca

McArthur Glen Designer Outlet

McArthur Glen Designer Outlet at Vancouver Airport, opened in summer 2015 on a 30-acre Sea Island site, is British Columbia's largest upscale designer Outlet. Conveniently located close to Vancouver International Airport along the Canada Line, the mall offers luxury European-style shopping experience.

Lulu Island Winery

Lulu Island Winery is a gold-medal winner and Canada's largest exporter of ice wine to China. Following a visit from Taiwan in 1992, Alison Lu and John Chang opened the doors to the winery in 2001. Today, they combine traditional Chinese winemaking methods with modern Western technology to produce a variety of wines. Local soil provides high quality blueberries and cranberries, while raspberries and grapes are from the Okanagan.

www.luluislandwinery.com

Canada Berries Winery

Canada Berries, located in East Richmond, is British Columbia's largest fruit winery, they offer a wide range of fruit and grape wines: blueberry, apple, strawberry, peach, blackcurrant, raspberry, rhubarb, white currant, cranberry, gooseberry, blackberry and more.

All berry fruits come directly from Fraser Valley or their blueberry farm. www.canadablueberries.com

Dining in Richmond

Chef Tony Seafood Restaurant
101-4600 No. 3 Rd. (within the Golden Village)
604.279.0083
www.cheftonycanada.com/en/

Blue Canoe Waterfront Restaurant

140-3866 Bayview Street

604.275.7811

www.bluecanoerestaurant.com

Hoi Tong Chinese Seafood Restaurant

8191 Westminster Hwy

604. 276.9229

Pajo's at Steveston on the Wharf

12351 3 Ave

604. 272.1588

www.pajos.com

Great River Fishing Adventures

Great River Fishing Adventures offers professional guide fishing charters on the Fraser River as well as many surrounding tributaries and lakes. These destinations include the Fraser, Pitt, Lillooet, and Columbia Rivers. In addition to salmon fishing, they offer fly fishing and single- and double-handed Spey fishing for sturgeon and steelhead. www.greatriverfishing.com

A Mary L. Peachin Adventure

Fraser River Sturgeon Fishing

Motoring upriver, we stopped to bottom fish at a place where the Harrison River flows into the Fraser. Guide Len Ames spotted a sturgeon on his fish finder. Chatting while we waited for the bite, we watched a pair of harbor seals fight over one of many spawning sockeye salmon headed up the river. A bald eagle and a flock of Canada geese fed along the shore while gulls flew overhead. The day was beautiful. It wasn't long before we would have plenty of action.

Photo credit Mary L. Peachin

Tom Bird and I were fishing for white sturgeon. Len told us that "during the past few years fishing guides along this stretch of the river have tagged 11,000 sturgeon. This season I have caught and released six tagged fish. This indicates to me that the sturgeon population is healthy and migrating."

Northern British Columbia Rockies' snowmelt flows into the Fraser River, a distance of 900 miles to its mouth in Sandhead. From a small trickle, muddy water flows into Steveston's delta. Here, the Fraser branches into a second arm at Point Roberts before reaching its mouth two miles offshore.

During spring and summer months, the river is a silty brown. Near banks, the bottom is covered with pebbles. Five species of Pacific salmon spawn in the Fraser River as well as Dolly Varden, cutthroat trout, migrating steelhead runs, and sturgeon.

Sturgeon have been known to migrate into the ocean as well as to stray into other river systems. They feed on salmon fry, oolichans, a smelt-like oil bearing fish, and lamprey eels.

A slow moving fish, a hooked sturgeon can erupt like a flash of lighting easily spooling a reel. They make long fast runs, and larger fish have been known to "tailwalk" across a river surface like marlin or sailfish. Those who think sturgeon fishing is like "pulling up a log" are misinformed. Many anglers who use to consider them a "coarse" fish now regard them as a sport fish.

As they often nibble before taking the bait, Len can recognize the bite of a sturgeon by the gentle technique. White sturgeon have four sucker-like barbels with scutes or spiny barbs bristling along the backs and sides of their bodies. Their wide toothless mouth makes them appear like they could use a set of dentures. Their jaw strength allows them to swallow prey whole. Like sharks, they are cartilaginous, or lacking a skeleton, and, also like sharks, they have denticles instead of scales.

While an average sturgeon released on the Fraser is between 4 to 4½ feet, the largest sturgeon, weighing more than 1,450 pounds, was caught sport fishing near Mission Bar dates in the 1950's. The prehistoric fish, which has no predators, date back 250 million years, prior to the age of dinosaurs.

They are a tremendous game fish, great sport, and protected by catch and release policies. Sturgeon mature slowly, approximately 12 years for males and 26 years for females, a good reason that they are fiercely protected.

After anchoring his 22-foot Chevy 310 horsepower Wooldridge on a "stable" current, Len baited the hooks with salmon roe mixed with other parts bound with a section of his wife's panty hose. Using heavy gear, 8½-foot fiberglass rods, 7-9 ought Mustad hooks, 130-pound test line with a 96# leader plus weights ranging from 4 to 22 ounces, we were ready for action.

Chatting as we waited for a bite, a pair of Harbor seals fought over one of the many sockeye salmon headed up the river to spawn. In a span of several hours, Tom and I each hooked and fought a sturgeon. While the strength of the fish is awesome, shallow the water, heavy line, and use of rod leverage allowed us to bring two 4-4½-footers to the boat in approximately 15 minutes. Larger sturgeon can take hours to release.

The record-breaking sturgeon was caught sport fishing near Mission Bar in the 50's. It weighed more than 1,450 pounds. Sturgeon have no predators.

A Mary L. Peachin Adventure

Vancouver Chinook Classic: A Pin Popping Screamer

The "red alert" broadcast email warned anglers, "it's going to be *brutal,* dress warmly, don't wear runners." Vancouver's weather forecast called for 100% chance of heavy rainfall and high wind. That would translate to a 100 millimeters of drenching rain. The deluge accompanied by 90-kilometer winds would produce horizontal precipitation.

Vancouver Chinook Classic Derby, an annual catch and release salmon tournament shouted out the forecast proclaiming finality, "The show must go on."

Thirty-three boats from British Columbia, carrying approximately 100 anglers, moored their boats at Richmond's host Pacific Gateway Hotel and Marina on the Fraser River.

After gathering at five in the morning for a "fisherman's breakfast", anxious anglers boarded their respective boats to motor along the Fraser River to Vancouver's harbor: gale force winds, rock and rolling choppy seas, and full moon strong currents. Our 26' Grady White captained by Mike Menten from Pacific Anglers was powered by two 150 HP Yamaha engine. We were one of the bigger boats.

My three fishing buddies included two local businessmen and photographer Todd Martin. The first "Pin popper screamer", a Chinook large enough to wrench the baited line out of the downrigger, occurred five minutes after lines were permitted in the water. I didn't hesitate when they, being gentlemen, said, "Ladies first". I saw the line pop out of the downrigger and the spool going wild. I knew that this fish might be a contender. As someone yelled, "Reel, reel, reel," I knew not to "horse" the fish and risk breaking the line.

If the Chinook wasn't large enough to win, it was certainly strong. Bringing the Chinook to the boat, Captain Mike concluded that it looked like a high "teener". Probably not a winning size, it would be a waste of time to call the weigh boat. Derbies are usually won by Chinook weighing 30 (called a tyee) or more pounds. In stormy conditions, it could take the "weigh" boat a half hour to arrive. During that wait time, the fish had to be held in the water and kept ALIVE. Focused more on the task at hand, I didn't protest not calling the weigh boat. Mike was probably correct except he didn't consider the weather and water conditions we would endure for the next 18 hours.

Downriggers with cannon balls lowered sardine-baited barbless hooks to various depths. Only a sizable Chinook can snap the line out of the downrigger clip as the whirring reel spools fast and loud. In order to be in prize contention, a "weigh" boat is called and volunteers measure the length and girth to determine the fish weight by formula. In these conditions, just getting the lines in the water was a challenge.

Fishing was slow and currents tangled lines. Four trolling lines were reduced to two. There was a miscommunication about food and water available on the boat. We were at the mercy of our growling stomachs for 12 hours. The food boat scheduled to bring out goodies to anglers couldn't handle the rough sea conditions.

We were fortunate to have a cover and a head, although it took us awhile to learn that the flusher was barely operative. A Gravol seasick pill saved one of our fishers who did not have a cast iron stomach. With only two seats, one occupied by the Captain, one angler wrapped his legs around me to hold me steady in the bow. He was so cold that his legs were shaking. The thought of his seasick barfing on my back dwelt in my mind. It was a very tough day of play with no entries to claim victory.

As conditions worsened, Vancouver's more distant areas were closed for fishing. When asked about the location of life jackets, Mike assured us that they were in the hatch. Not so comforting when cold-water hypothermia can kill in minutes. We felt minimal relief seeing the Coast Guard hovering nearby. Some boats lost equipment, others simply returned to the Marina. Remaining boats fished English Bay, Vancouver Harbor, Georgia Strait, T10, the yellow bell buoy, and the North arm of the Fraser.

Lines up! Returning to the Pacific Gateway late in the afternoon, all was dark. The worse summer storm in a decade, maybe the worse summer storm ever, had battered the Lower Mainland, toppling drought-stricken trees into houses, cars, power lines. It would be several days before residents between metro-Vancouver and Seattle, Washington had power fully restored. The winning fish the first day was a mere 23 pounds. More regrets that I hadn't insisted on calling the weigh boat. The $25,000 prize would not be mine.

The angling fiasco continued on the next day. Logs used for pulp were tied in the Fraser River and floated over their barriers, creating "dead head" hazards for boaters. It was a slalom course to the harbor.

The second day was shorter, but rougher. Between strong currents and chop it was bone jarring, arm-bruising troughs. Calls to the weigh boat were minimal. Then, a frantic call was heard 10 minutes before the Derby ended at 1 PM. David Wei fishing on a Pacific Angler boat landed a 23 pound Chinook. With a pin popping screamer, he snatched the title with minutes to spare.

Certified Tidal Angling Guides

Carl Archibald, Vancouver Island, Victoria, carl_archibald@hotmail.com

Chad Calder, Coquitlam, Coast Wide Sports Fishing

Dan Harvey, Vancouver Island, Port Renfrew, Pacific Sportfishing Charters

Dave Hunchak, Vancouver Island, Campbell River, hunchaks@telus.net

Dennis Kaechele, Vancouver Island, Merville, pacificwild@hotmail.com

Dave Korsch, Vancouver Coast and Mountains, Gibsons, Predator Charters

Cameron McCulloch, Vancouver Island, Duncan, cammuck@hotmail.com

Bill Murray, Vancouver Island, Courtney, fishshack17@gmail.com

Don H. Parrish, Vancouver Island, Campbell River, donhparrish@hotmail.com

Chris Ranger, Vancouver Island, Port Hardy, ranger@telus.net

Curtis Smith, Vancouver Island, Campbell River, Coastal Wilderness Adventures

List Of Contributors

Canfisco Corporation, Don McLeod

Charlotte Queen Adventures, Jill Fincher

Coastal Island Fishing Adventures, Gary Stotts

Critter Cove Marina, Cameron and Catherine Forbes

Dolphins North Lodge, Clint Cameron

Dolphins Resort Vancouver Island, Clint Cameron

Duncanby Lodge, Sid Keay, Chris Wu, Joann Broadhead, John Cox

Duval Point Lodge, David and Lisa Beckman

Elk River, Michael Delich, Bill Wilcox, Elk River Guiding Company, Louis Cloutier

Fairmont Hotels, Philip Barnes, Nanci Hall, Julie Melanson

Foggy Point Charter Services, Rodney Proskiw

Fraser River Lodge, Frank Staiger

Great River Fishing Adventures, Matthew Clive

Homefray Lodge Desolation Sound, Scott Macey

Langara Fishing Adventures, Mike Randall, Karen Trapp

Murphy Sportfishing, David and Marilyn Murphy

Nootka Island Lodge, Tim Cyr

Northern British Columbia Tourism, Susan Clarke, Regional Media Relations

Ole's Hakai Pass, Ernie Daley, Joan Comeau

Pacific Gateway Hotel, Donald Pinkney

Pacific Salmon Foundation, Cory Matheson

Pacific Sport Fishing Charters, Dan Harvey

Peregrine Lodge, Bruce McFadden

Predator Charters, David Korsch

Protected Water Charters, Harley Elias

Rivers Inlet Sportsman's Club, Barbara Kelly

Rosewood Georgia Hotel, Matt Laurel

Rugged Point Lodge, Kristy and Matt Guiguet

Shearwater Resort, Shawn Nagurny, Mike Maenck

Skeena Spey Lodge, Jeroen Wohe

Sonora Resort, Sohia Cheng, Wendy Hartley

Sport Fishing Institute, Owen Bird

Sport Fishing Magazine, Editor-in-Chief Doug Olander

Sunds Lodge, Scott Sund

The Lodge at Gold River, Kent O'Neill, Jayne Lloyd Jones

Tofino, Vancouver Island, Charles McDiarmid, The Wickininnish Inn

Tourism Richmond, Michelle Dunn, Tracy Lakeman, Laura Roberts

Tourism Victoria, Amanda Eyolfson

Ucluelet, Caleb Cameron, Cameron Sport Fishing

West Coast Fishing Club, Rick Grange, Brian Grange, Terry Cowan, Chris Dale

West Sport Fishing, George and Lisa Cuthbert

Westcoast Fishing Adventures, Gil and Mandi McKean

Westcoast Resorts, Brian Alexander, Shawna McKay, Paul Cain

www.lastcastguiding.com, Pat Ahern

Westwind Tugboat Adventures, Wayne Kellett

About The Author

Photo credit PK Weis

Mary L. Peachin, a native Tucsonan, divides her time between Arizona and the city of Vancouver. Author of *The Complete Idiots' Guide to Sharks* (Alpha/Penguin), *Scuba Caribbean* (University Press Florida), *Sport Fishing in the Caribbean* (Amazon Kindle) plus several updates, Mary has been a longtime angler.

Originally invited to British Columbia by the late Sport Fishing Institute Executive Director Tom Bird to experience its sport fishing, she fell in love with the province as well as the diversification of British Columbia's sport fishing and uniqueness of its lodges

Mary is a longtime active member of the International Women's Fishing Association. She has been honored with two annual awards for releasing Chinook salmon and rainbow trout. Her freelance fishing stories have been featured in many United States newspapers and magazines. She has been recognized and honored by the Rocky Mountain Chapter of the Outdoor Writer's of America for her fishing articles and photographs.

When Mary is not fishing, her passion is scuba diving. Her freelance writing and photography have taken her to all seven continents, and she has written about them all.